Weekend Walks

on the Delmarva Peninsula

Atlantic breakers pound old observation towers in Cape Henlopen State Park, Delaware. The tall lookouts were used during World War II to spot enemy vessels and direct the fire of shore batteries near the mouth of the Delaware Bay.

Weekend Walks

on the Delmarva Peninsula

Walks and Hikes in Delaware and the Eastern
Shore of Maryland and Virginia

Second Edition

Jay Abercrombie

The Countryman Press
Woodstock, Vermont

An Invitation to the Reader

Although it is unlikely that these tours will change much with time, some road signs, landmarks, and other terms may. If you find that changes have occurred on these routes, please let us know so we may correct them in future editions. Address all correspondence to:

Editor
Weekend Walks series
The Countryman Press
P.O. Box 748
Woodstock, VT 05091

Library of Congress Cataloging-in-Publication
Data has been applied for.

ISBN-10: 0-88150-667-2
ISBN-13: 978-0-88150-667-9

Published by The Countryman Press, P.O. Box 748, Woodstock, VT 05091

Distributed by W. W. Norton & Company, Inc., 500 Fifth Avenue, New York, NY 10110

Cover design by Dede Cummings Designs
Text design by Chelsea Designs
Composition by Kelly Thompson
Cover photograph of the Oyster Chaff Trail spanning a tidal stream
    in Maryland's Terrapin Nature Park by Jay Abercrombie
Maps by Moore Creative Designs
Interior photographs by the author

Printed in the United States of America

10 9 8 7 6 5 4 3 2 1

Weekend Walks on the Delmarva Peninsula
is dedicated to my dad, George Abercrombie

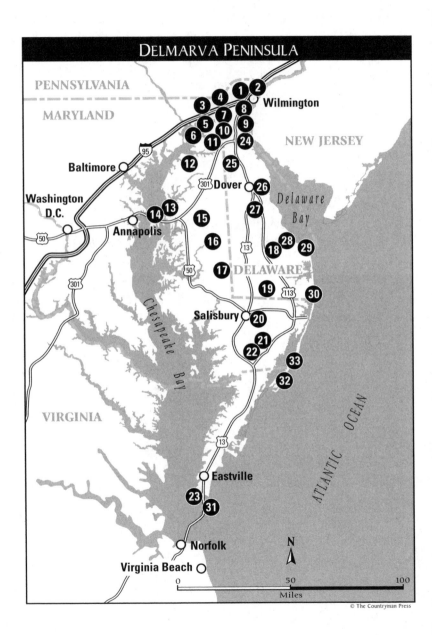

Contents

Acknowledgments

During the time required to write this guidebook, I was helped by many people who provided information and encouragement. Most of these people I had met only for the first time, and most were hikers who took a personal interest in making this book a fact.

I am grateful to everyone who contributed to the completion of this guide. I want to make special mention of the following. Charles Salkin, Delaware Division of Parks and Recreation, originally conceived the idea of a hiking guide to the Delmarva Peninsula. He made available all his preliminary notes and was always eager to answer questions, provide information, or explore a new trail with me. Eileen Butler, also of the Delaware Division of Parks and Recreation, helped me with maps and information about Delaware's natural heritage. All staff members of the Delaware state parks gave complete cooperation during my visits. Special thanks for their personal efforts and hospitality go to Michael Felker (Lums Pond), Donald Ott (Cape Henlopen), Barbara Woodford (Brandywine Creek), and Dave Hyson (Port Penn).

Forester James Dobson helped with Blackbird State Forest. Katy O'Connell provided invaluable help on the Delaware National Estuarine Research Reserve in general and Saint Jones Reserve in particular. Brian Cannon and Joan Foster of the New Castle Court House Museum interpreted New Castle's long and complex history.

In Maryland, I was fortunate to have assistance from Nita Settina of the Maryland Park Service. The state lands on the Eastern Shore are ably cared for by many dedicated managers, foresters, and rangers, including Scott Smith, John Ohler (Tuckahoe, Martinak, and Sassafras), Bill Yates (Pocomoke River), Roy Miller (Pocomoke), Mike Schofield (Wicomico),

Shawn Day (Elk Neck State Forest), and Gino Clark (Elk Neck State Park). Joe Reinhardt shared his considerable knowledge of Native Americans with me. Gregg Todd, Deputy Director of the Queen Anne's County Department of Parks and Recreation, provided maps and information on Terrapin Nature Park. Doug Samson, The Nature Conservancy, was always available to answer another question on Delmarva bays or other specialized habitats.

Staff members of the U.S. Fish and Wildlife Service cooperated fully during my work on national wildlife refuges, especially Bill J. Jones (Prime Hook), Allison Penn (Chincoteague), and Tom Eagle (Eastern Neck). Ethan Kimbrough, National Park Service, helped me explore Assateague Island.

To my editor, Glenn Novak, I owe many thanks for his help and patience through numerous revisions. Kermit Hummel, editorial director, Jennifer Thompson, managing editor, and Clare Innes, production co-ordinator at the Countryman Press, offered encouragement, advice, and assistance at every step.

Many friends and associates provided inspiration and gave generously of their time and knowledge as I wrote this guide. Special thanks must go to Debbi Snook, Tom Earley, Jean Merson, Kathleen Bradley, Sandy Garey, Charles Darling, Laura DeYoung, Bob and Ruth Brown, Mark Scallion, Lisa Daiber, Dana Zintek, and Keith Clancy. Finally, I thank my son-in-law Thomas Huynh, who provided valuable help when inevitable computer problems arose.

Introduction

The Delmarva Peninsula is a sharply defined piece of land along the Atlantic Coast. Geographically, ecologically, historically, culturally, and politically, it is unique among the regions of the United States. Dangling like a cluster of grapes from the mainland, the peninsula is bordered by the Susquehanna River and Chesapeake Bay on the west and by the Delaware River, Delaware Bay, and North Atlantic Ocean on the east. The northern boundary is the Mason-Dixon Line separating Delaware and Maryland from Pennsylvania. The peninsula narrows at the shoulders but broadens to a wide girth before tapering precipitously to its southernmost point at Cape Charles.

Three states share the peninsula—Delaware, Maryland, and Virginia. Combining parts of their names results in *Delmarva*. All of Delaware lies on the peninsula, occupying only about 33 percent of the land area but holding approximately 64 percent of its people. Most of the population is centered around Wilmington in the north. Part of Maryland occupies more than half the land area of the peninsula. Nine counties (from north to south: Cecil, Kent, Queen Anne's, Caroline, Talbot, Dorchester, Wicomico, Worcester, and Somerset) comprise the Maryland Eastern Shore, that part of the state east of the Chesapeake Bay. The Virginia Eastern Shore is sparsely populated and contains only two counties: Accomack and Northampton.

The Delmarva Peninsula covers almost 6,000 square miles. It is over 200 miles long and at its greatest width is approximately 70 miles across. About 1.3 million people live on Delmarva, but the population is

Maryland's Terrapin Nature Park bridges acres of salt marsh and maritime forest and preserves almost one mile of the Chesapeake Bay shore.

unevenly distributed. Most live in the north, particularly in Wilmington, Newark, and Elkton. Smaller urban cores occur around Dover and Salisbury. The seaside resorts of Rehoboth Beach, Bethany Beach, Ocean City, and Chincoteague become crowded with large numbers of tourists in the summer.

Almost the entire peninsula lies on the Atlantic Coastal Plain, a land noteworthy for its flatness. Here, in the maritimes, you are seldom far from water. Even the uplands of the Coastal Plain on Delmarva are frequently swampy. Wide, deep, tidal rivers indent the Maryland Chesapeake shore. The rivers and the far-spreading marshes tend to isolate towns and communities. It is sometimes shorter to travel by water than by land between two points. On the Delaware shore, short rivers and creeks curl through the tidal marshes to empty into the Delaware Bay or into shallow, brackish lagoons. Beginning in Maryland and extending south through

Virginia, the mainland lies behind outer, low, barrier islands and narrow bays.

Most of the hikes in this book are on the Coastal Plain. They reach into virtually every available habitat: upland oak-pine forests of willow oak, pin oak, post oak, Spanish oak, loblolly pine, scrub pine, and pitch pine; bottomland swamps of bald cypress, black gum, overcup oak, and red maple; salt marshes; islands bordering the rivers, bays, and ocean; sandy beaches; dunes; isolated hilltops; and even man-made environments such as old millponds, a canal, and historic towns.

The Coastal Plain is largely an area of prosperous farms and water-man communities. The peninsula below the northern megalopolis is mostly rural and agrarian. The rich farmland is interspersed with iso-lated wild areas preserved along marshy creeks or set aside as state parks and forests. Wildlife is abundant and diverse, and plant life is rich and luxuriant, adding a sense of excitement and wonder to almost any hike. Walking is the right tempo for experiencing this land, often overlooked by car travelers as they speed between home and the ocean beaches.

At the extreme northern edge of Delmarva, the landscape changes dra-matically. Here, beyond the fall line, is a small area of low, rolling hills and swift-flowing streams—the Piedmont. Delmarva's highest elevations occur here. The first four hikes in this guidebook (Brandywine Creek State Park, Bellevue State Park, Fair Hill Natural Resources Management Area, and White Clay Creek State Park) are in the Piedmont. The walks over this terrain are steeper and sometimes more rugged than those on the Coastal Plain. They traverse rich woodlands of oak, hickory, tulip tree, and beech often interspersed by open meadows and old fields.

The biggest cities and heaviest industry occur near the fall line and into the Piedmont, yet some of the best hiking is found here. The gentle hills and rounded valleys offer refreshing variety amid a scenic setting home to eastern chipmunk and red squirrel. On hot summer days, the cool shade of the thick forests provides a welcome environment for a walk.

The Delmarva trails allow you to escape the cares and troubled thoughts of civilization. No matter the season or the weather, you can become immersed in the natural sights and sounds surrounding you. Kingfishers flash from tree to tree along a creek. The true winter call of the blue jay resounds from a tangle of shrubs. Here, at the edge of the woods, birds send whistled messages to each other, warning of your approach. The soft rushing of water, the sighing of wind in the trees, the noise of your own feet on the trail are sounds that, once experienced, will remain with you for a lifetime. Years later, in reverie, you can look at a map and point to one spot or another and immediately be there.

Delmarva lies in a transition zone for vegetation and is at the northern limit for several species of southern plants. Bald cypress, loblolly pine, redbay, and sweetleaf reach their northernmost stands on the peninsula. Other southern species, such as magnolias, sweet gum, tall pawpaw, American mistletoe, American holly, and tulip tree, are common. Delmarva also claims a few indigenous plants of its own. For example, some hybridization among oaks has been found where the coastal species meet the Piedmont species. Seaside alder is endemic to Delaware and the Eastern Shore of Maryland. Unusual nontidal freshwater ponds, called Delmarva bays, are found in a small area of the peninsula. They harbor rare plants and animals that are specially adapted to complete their life cycles in these seasonally flooded habitats.

Some southern animals, especially invertebrates such as insects and clams, are also at their northern range limits in the region. Delmarva is noted as an important haven for wildlife. The rare eastern tiger salamander is found only in Kent County, Maryland on the peninsula, where it breeds in a few isolated ponds. The endangered Delmarva fox squirrel is found nowhere else on earth. Threatened birds of prey, especially bald eagle and peregrine falcon, occur here in encouraging numbers. Waterfowl and wading birds are plentiful. The overwintering populations of ducks, geese, and swans on the peninsula and adjacent waters provide a spectacle of wild America equaled in very few other locations.

Throughout your walks, you will be aware of the rich historical heritage of this land. Little evidence of the original inhabitants remains, but their influence lives on in the place names of rivers, islands, and bays:

Chincoteague, Assateague, Assawoman, Sinepuxent, Chesapeake, Tuckahoe, Pocomoke, Nanticoke, Susquehanna, Choptank, Annemessex, and Indian River. Layered over the ancient native civilizations is the more recent heritage of European colonization. Vestiges of Swedish and Dutch colonial days can be found in Delaware, but most of Delmarva has a decidedly English flavor. Names of towns and other governmental jurisdictions reflect this tradition: Sussex, Princess Anne, Queen Anne's, Queenstown, Cambridge, Oxford, Centreville, Dover, New Castle, and Royal Oak.

This English heritage permeates most of rural Delmarva south of the urbanized sector. Linguists report that the native accents resemble the English spoken during the Elizabethan age (1558–1603). The area's isolation disappears a little more each day, but the peninsula remains one of the last, truly idiosyncratic parts of the United States, ranking with coastal Maine, southern Louisiana, Texas west of the Pecos, and outlying parts of Hawaii and Alaska. The people are a tough, old-fashioned breed, secure in their convictions and self-sufficient in their ways, content to be left alone but also friendly and helpful.

How to Use This Book

This trail guide is divided into three geographical areas: The North, Chesapeake Bay, and Delaware Bay/Atlantic Ocean. Each region offers a wide variety of different scenery and unique qualities, an unexpected surprise for such a relatively small area. There is no need to walk the trails in sequence. Each chapter is designed to stand alone. Simply pick out a hike suitable to your time, circumstances, and interests.

Each chapter provides a complete description of a hike, detailed instructions on how to reach the trailhead from a county seat or other nearby large town, and a commentary on the area's natural or human history. A capsule highlight of what can be seen is provided at the beginning of each hike's description, along with the distance and an estimated walking time. The latter figure is an average that tries to allow time for lingering over woodland wildflowers, sudden sightings of wildlife, or moments spent contemplating a grand landscape.

Also listed at the outset is the U.S. Geological Survey (USGS) 7.5-minute quadrangle map or maps showing the area of the hike. When available, other maps (such as those published by state parks) that show the area or the trails are also mentioned. All these maps are listed only to provide you with more detailed information if desired. They are not specifically needed to follow the trails, since sketch maps of each hike are pictured in the book. Other useful references include the DeLorme Atlas and Gazetteer (Maryland/Delaware and Virginia editions) and the National Geographic Trails Illustrated map of the Delmarva Peninsula.

Hiking on Delmarva is possible during all four seasons. Most winter days are warm and sunny; snowfalls are generally light and short-lived. Many people find winter the ideal season to be on the trail because they avoid the heat, ticks, and biting insects of summer. Warm weather walks, on the other hand, can be especially scenic and pleasant. Summer is rich with color and activity in nature, while spring and autumn offer the vibrant changes in which all living things become immersed.

The Trails

Most of the hikes in this book are along marked and maintained trails, but some are on paths with no markings or signs. These latter hikes often follow forest roads, firebreaks, shorelines, or informal paths, so bush-whacking is seldom necessary.

I believe it is impossible to get lost for long in any of these areas; civilization is never far away. If you should become temporarily disoriented, take comfort in Francis Bacon's sage advice ("He that follows nature is never lost"), and you will soon come upon a road or watercourse.

All trails in the book except one are day walks and can be classed as easy to moderate in difficulty (even those in the Piedmont). The lone, long, backpacking trip on Assateague Island is a rigorous hike requiring experience, skill, and stamina—a challenge testing your leg muscles and nerve.

Three long-distance footpaths are of particular interest to hikers. The Brandywine Trail runs through the Brandywine Valley of Delaware and

Pennsylvania. A segment of this trail that is on public land is described in the chapter on Brandywine Creek State Park. The Mason-Dixon Trail connects the Brandywine Trail with the Appalachian Trail. It weaves along the borders of Delaware, Maryland, and Pennsylvania. Hikes in White Clay Creek State Park, Elk Neck State Forest, and on Iron Hill cover parts of the Mason-Dixon Trail. The American Discovery Trail begins in Cape Henlopen State Park and stretches across the continent to the Pacific Ocean in California. You can hike a short stretch of the American Discovery Trail in the hike described in the chapter on Tuckahoe State Park.

Beach Walking

Hikers on the Delmarva Peninsula are truly fortunate for the many opportunities for beach walking. Beaches are much more open than the flat woodlands of Delmarva, and you can see for miles along them. William H. Amos has called walking on a wild beach "a splendid isolation that separates you from the rest of the world and returns you to the natural —even primeval earth. It is as though you were the only person in the world, walking upon pristine sands that bear no tread of any living creatures, leaving behind footprints that as surely as the tide rises will soon be erased forever."

Clearly, hikes along beaches bordering the ocean, the bays, and the tidal rivers and creeks add a dimension to walking that cannot be gained in forested mountains or rocky hills. All or part of the following hikes in this guide are along a variety of beautiful, often uncrowded, beaches: Elk Neck State Park, Old New Castle Historic District, Pea Patch Island, Sassafras Natural Resources Management Area, Eastern Neck Island, Terrapin Nature Park, Kiptopeke State Park, Cape Henlopen State Park, Fenwick Island State Park, Chincoteague National Wildlife Refuge, and Assateague Island.

Beach walking, however, requires some special preparation and considerations, based largely upon common sense. In the summer, sunscreen combined with sunglasses and a hat are necessary to prevent undue exposure to the sun. If barefoot, be careful to avoid sharp shells, rocks, jellyfish, or worse, broken bottles cast up on the shore. Also, remember to apply sunscreen to your feet; nothing can ruin an outing worse than sunburned feet. Carry repellent in your pack in case biting insects become bothersome. Consider carrying a pair of lightweight sneakers or wading shoes, a swimsuit, and a beach towel.

In spring and summer, some beaches as well as the dunes just behind them may be nesting sites for shorebirds. Avoid entering these areas, and keep your dog from ranging through the colonies. Birds such as plovers, terns, and skimmers are under great pressure from shore development, off-road vehicles (ORVs), and just the sheer number of people on the beach. Their nesting success in recent years has greatly diminished. They need our help. Some land use agencies may post warning signs or close some stretches of beach to human use to protect nesting birds or other species. Whether or not warning signs are posted, watch for any nesting activity and give wide berth.

Beach walking in cold weather can be especially rewarding because few people are out and you can be truly alone with the sea and the sand. Mild winter days along the Delmarva coast are ideal for hiking. Even quite severe weather should be no hindrance to your walking if you are properly clothed against the chill wind and spume that may blow off the water. Although a winter beach can be astonishingly beautiful, it also can be punishingly cold.

Clothing, Gear, and Safety

Experience will determine the best clothing for your day hikes. I usually wear hiking boots, even for relatively short hikes, but comfortable sneakers are fine for most walks in this book. Backpacking always requires boots. Wear footgear you do not mind getting wet or muddy. I frequently walk barefoot on beaches but carry sneakers in my day pack in case I encounter woodland, brush, or rough terrain.

I ordinarily wear shorts in the spring, summer, and autumn. They are much cooler and I can often feel or see ticks as they crawl up my legs. However, some of my hiking friends think long pants tucked into high boots should be worn in tick country. This approach, combined with a tick repellent, is necessary if you expect to encounter hundreds of ticks— a possible occurrence on the peninsula during certain seasons. Shorts also become a disadvantage when biting insects are numerous, because so much more skin is exposed to their attacks.

I usually carry a light pack for stowing my gear—lunch, water in a plastic bottle (water from Delmarva ponds and streams is unsafe to drink), and perhaps a rain parka or a swimsuit depending on the weather outlook. This guidebook is designed to fit easily into your pack; take it with you on the trail. One other very important item for Delmarva walks is insect repellent. A separate little first aid kit containing a few bandages and moleskin for foot blisters is a good idea. You also may consider any of the following as appropriate for your pack, depending on the trail and weather: knife, matches, flashlight, compass, space blanket, sunglasses. I also like to carry lightweight binoculars and perhaps a field guide or two to identify flora and fauna.

Delmarva enjoys a long tradition of the shooting sports. Hunting is permitted on most public lands, and you must be aware of legal hunting seasons when planning your walks. Keep in mind that hunting usually occurs from dawn to dusk, from Monday through Saturday, and on various dates from mid-September through January and from mid-April to mid-May. The federal and three state agencies responsible for natural resources on the peninsula have different policies regarding use of parks, forests, and other public lands during various hunting seasons. Some agencies close parts of parks and sections of trails to all but hunters, while others allow unlimited access to all users. Regulations also vary depending on the type of hunting season (for example, waterfowl, small game, or large game).

Most regulations for hunters require them to wear protectively colored clothing while pursuing their quarry. Use common sense and do the same if you plan to hike during hunting season. Gear for you and all members of your group should include at a minimum caps of solid daylight fluorescent orange color and vests or jackets containing back and front panels of solid fluorescent orange color. The Maryland Department of Natural Resources recommends that your vest or jacket should have at least 250 square inches of orange. Your day pack, too, should be marked with protective orange fluorescence. Fluorescent orange coats and collars for dogs are also available. If possible, plan your hikes for Sundays during hunting season; the states on the peninsula do not permit hunting on Sundays. The introduction to each chapter discusses any restrictions or warnings about hunting that you need to consider.

The only poisonous snake recorded on the Delmarva Peninsula is northern copperhead, but it is considered rare. Count yourself lucky if you see a snake of any species on your walks; I can remember observing only a few during my many outings. Like most wild creatures, they scurried away quickly.

Hiking Programs and Entrance Fees

The opportunities for hiking on Delmarva have expanded greatly in the last decade or so. New parks and forests have been established and new trails have been built. The increased availability of footpaths is in response to people using existing trails and asking for more places to hike. More than 97 percent of those responding to the Virginia Outdoor Survey in 2000 rated trails as the most important offering state parks provide.

Delaware State Parks sponsors the Trail Challenge, a free program designed to reward hikers who walk a complete set of trails in state parks throughout the First State. The current plan calls for hiking 15 designated trails, measuring almost 40 miles, in one year. Successful hikers receive a certificate and a patch. More information is available at any of the Delaware State Parks featured in this book.

The Maryland Forest Service and the Maryland Park Service use the Trail Stewardship Program to increase funding for trail maintenance and growth. For a minimum $5 tax deductible donation, you receive a window sticker and periodic mailings with information on trail use, volunteer opportunities, and upcoming trail projects. You have the option of designating your donation to the forest or park where your favorite trails are located. You can join at any forest or park office featured in this guide.

Some of the trails in this book are on public lands that charge an entrance fee. Rules vary, but generally admission is levied at Delaware State Parks, Virginia State Parks, some Maryland State Parks, and some federal sites. Delaware and Maryland charge nonresidents an extra fee. Some parks do not charge admission in the off-season, although the areas remain open. Consider purchasing an annual pass from the states or from the federal government that will grant you entrance to all applicable parks for an entire year or longer at a considerable cost savings. All agencies offer discounts to older citizens and Delaware extends this discount to people who are on active duty with the military.

Conservation

No virgin land remains on Delmarva, except possibly a few acres of remote salt marsh on Bombay Hook National Wildlife Refuge. Nevertheless, much of wild Delmarva still exists or has been restored through good conservation measures after decades of neglect. Hikers, who have a deep concern for the land, air, and water so vital to life, have much to celebrate. You can explore some of the East's most beautiful and pristine landscapes on the trails described in this guide. You have good chances to see bald eagles at many places on the peninsula. Snow geese, uncommon in the 1960s, exceed 100,000 adults each winter. Stocks of rockfish, the state fish of Maryland, were at alarmingly low levels until recent quotas were put into place. Now rockfish charity tournaments are held and some landed fish weigh more than 30 pounds.

Significant progress has been made in preserving and restoring Delmarva's ecosystems, but much remains to be done. It sometimes seems unjust when you return to a favorite woodland where you walked last spring and the area is clear-cut, or when a familiar, winding stream is now imprisoned in banks of concrete, or when a wetland is drained. Recently, each year has seen fewer canvasbacks, Atlantic horseshoe crabs, and marine turtles. Approximately one-fourth of all plant species native to the Delmarva Peninsula have disappeared since 1900. The catch of Atlantic blue crab from the Chesapeake is near an all-time low. About 100 acres of the Chesapeake Bay watershed is converted from forests and wetlands to housing developments and shopping areas *each day*. Maryland suffers the highest rate of deforestation of any state east of the Mississippi.

Walking through nature helps us see the interconnectedness of all life. In our efforts to conserve a bit of open space for trails, we encounter problems such as toxic waste disposal, water pollution, water management, acid rain, and multiple use on public lands. Ultimately, every act we take to further conserve our natural resources—by making our own backyard or woodlot hospitable to wildlife, by saving a salt marsh, by improving an antipollution law, by modifying a forest management plan, by increasing appropriations for parks and refuges, by developing a comprehensive energy conservation plan—helps insure that there will be unbroken, undeveloped, wild, and rough places to roam. The trail ahead still harbors unpredictable and refreshing surprises. It still leads us on.

The North

White Clay Creek State Park

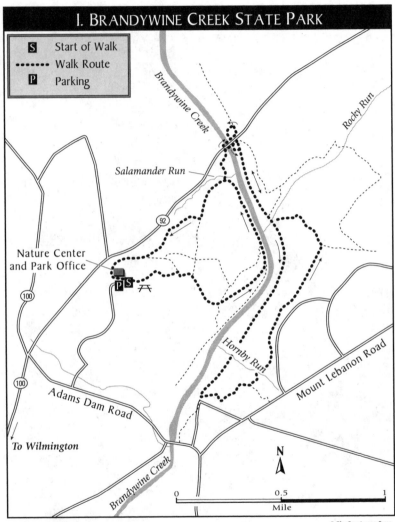

1. BRANDYWINE CREEK STATE PARK

S Start of Walk

•••••• Walk Route

P Parking

Brandywine Creek

Rocky Run

Salamander Run

92

Nature Center
and Park Office

100

P S

Hornby Run

100

Adams Dam Road

Mount Lebanon Road

To Wilmington

Brandywine Creek

N

0   0.5   1
Mile

© The Countryman Press

I. Brandywine Creek State Park

Magnificent plant life, including unmatched trees and luxuriant wildflowers

Hiking distance: 6 miles
Hiking time: 3 hours
Maps: USGS Wilmington North; park map

The Piedmont in Delaware is a highly scenic land of low, gently rolling hills and fertile valleys. Streams ripple over the countryside, and occasional outcrops of resistant rock indicate that this area is an inland setting, removed both geologically and geographically from the overriding influences of the sea. Only the northern perimeter of Delaware enters the Piedmont; the zone is scarcely 10 miles across at its widest in the state. It is Delaware's most densely populated sector; Wilmington and its suburbs have expanded into the former woods, fields, and farms. The area is characterized by a semiurban flavor, but the serene beauty of the Piedmont can still be experienced in the remaining open spaces—now the sites of estates, preserves, and parks.

Four of Delaware's 15 state parks are in the Piedmont. Brandywine Creek State Park preserves an especially picturesque section of a Piedmont valley noted for its scenery, history, and culture. Most of the land in the present-day park was owned from the early 1800s to the 1960s by the du Pont family. The wooded portions of the area have been relatively undisturbed for almost the past two hundred years. The tall trees are spectacular. Albert E. Radford, professor of botany at the University of North Carolina and a leading authority on Piedmont ecosystems, wrote, "[The] Brandywine Creek . . . forest is the most beautiful high-canopied woody community in the entire Piedmont"—a remarkable claim considering the Piedmont covers 85,000 square miles and stretches for 1,000 miles from

New Jersey to Alabama. Complementing the forest giants is a rich assortment of wildflowers that color the woodland floor and surrounding meadows each spring. Some three hundred species of wildflowers are recorded here.

The great trees are the glory of the park, but a man-made feature also deserves special mention—the artistic stone walls crisscrossing the meadows and forests. Built more than a century ago by Italians brought to this country to construct the DuPont Company mills along the Brandywine, they are such superb examples of the stonemason's art that they seem to be part of the land and add to the tranquility of the environment.

Your trail follows two loops through mature forests, old fields, and riverine habitats, passing by stone fences and a floodplain oxbow to cross Brandywine Creek on a highway bridge. The hike uses parts of seven named trails and a couple of connecting paths to cover 6 miles of the approximately 12 miles of trails in the park. Start at the Brandywine Creek Nature Center and initially follow a short segment of the interpretive Tulip Tree Trail. Pamphlets describing the numbered stations along the way may be available in the nature center, which is open 8:30–4:30 Sunday through Saturday.

Access

From downtown Wilmington, drive north on DE 52 for 2.7 miles. Turn right (north) on DE 100. In 2.4 miles come upon a crossroads where DE 100 turns to the left, DE 92 goes straight, and a side road enters from the right. Turn onto the side road (Adams Dam Road) and drive just 0.2 mile to the entrance of Brandywine Creek State Park on the left. An entrance fee is charged from May 1 to October 31. Follow the park road 0.7 mile, always keeping left at forks, until it dead-ends in the Brandywine Creek Nature Center parking lot.

The white-blazed Brandywine Trail stretches for 35 miles through the Brandywine Valley of Delaware and Pennsylvania. The segment in Brandywine Creek State Park is canopied by tall tulip trees.

Trail

"Enter this wild wood and view the haunts of Nature." William Cullen Bryant's invitation could well have been written about the beginning of this walk through the Tulip Tree Woods Nature Preserve.

Follow the path around the right of the nature center and continue straight through the break in the stone fence on the Tulip Tree Trail. This path wanders for 0.75 mile through the 24-acre nature preserve set aside to protect the majestic trees. The red-blazed Hidden Pond Trail and the yellow-blazed Indian Springs Trail share the same path. Just beyond station 4, the Tulip Tree Trail veers left at a fork. Keep right on the Hidden Pond and Indian Springs Trails.

The route soon leaves the nature preserve through a corner break in the stone wall and enters a much younger, scrubbier forest. The two trails split; keep right on the yellow-blazed Indian Springs Trail. Your way is canopied by shrubs and saplings as it follows an old road around a hillside.

The way drops gradually into the bottomland of Brandywine Creek. It curves left where a side trail comes in from the right rear and follows the creek. You are now walking upstream on the right bank.

The Hidden Pond Trail intersects from the left and continues straight ahead along the creek bank. The Indian Springs Trail turns left and climbs. Here keep straight on the Hidden Pond Trail and stay in the valley. Soon you pass by rocky cliffs that rise above the floodplain.

After the Hidden Pond Trail veers to the left away from the creek, an unmarked side trail goes off to the right and crosses Salamander Run on a long, wooden bridge. Follow this side trail for the second loop of today's walk; you will return to this spot later.

Beyond the footbridge, your path passes by Hidden Pond, a quiet oxbow nestled in a remnant of the old creek bed. The trail comes out upon DE 92; cross the highway, turn right, and walk over Brandywine Creek. On the other side of the bridge, turn left off the highway onto a paved trail. Immediately curve left and follow the broad trail that descends to pass under the span. You are now walking downstream on the left bank.

The way climbs slightly to reach the Thompsons Bridge area of the park. Continue downstream on an old, unpaved roadway known as the Creek Road. White blazes on trees along here indicate you are on the Brandywine Trail, a long-distance hiking path maintained by the Wilmington Trail Club. Running from Wilmington north into Pennsylvania, it largely traverses private lands (at least in Delaware); passage across these sections is restricted to members of the club or to hikers escorted by club members. Here in the park, the Brandywine Trail is open to everyone. The former road is also the route for the Northern Delaware Greenway Trail and the park's Creek Road Trail and Rocky Run Trail. A picnic area stretches along the banks of the creek.

At the crossing of Rocky Run, the first leg of the Rocky Run Trail turns left to climb the ridge. The main stem of the Rocky Run Trail continues straight a short distance to cross the tributary, and then the trail's second leg turns left to follow Rocky Run upstream. You will return to this spot later, but for now continue straight on the wide Brandywine/Northern Delaware

Greenway/Creek Road Trails. The tulip trees along the route rival those in the nature preserve for size and majesty.

Cross Hornby Run. Beyond, on a terrace on the right is a bank of signs about the creek's geological history. Just past the exhibit, the way reaches a pasture on the left and a young forest with noticeably smaller trees on the right. Before the pasture, an unmarked side trail enters from the left rear. Turn left and climb, leaving the old Creek Road behind.

The narrow path climbs steadily. Turn left at the first cross trail; the unmarked way is more or less level as it winds below the ridge crest through a stunning upland forest of tulip tree, northern red oak, and beech. Mountain laurel dominates the shrub layer. Cross a boulder-strewn streambed— the upper reaches of Hornby Run—and later another boulder field. Old stone walls, mostly tumbled down and weathered, are favorite haunts for eastern chipmunks.

Your trail rises to join with a sanitary sewer line, runs along the right-of-way for a short distance, and then drops to the left. The path reaches a T-junction with the Rocky Run Trail. Turn left and descend. The route is rough and rocky through the forest, but the way grows easier as you skirt a meadow and then pass through a plantation of big white pines. Come again to the old Creek Road near the bridge that spans Rocky Run. Turn right and retrace your way, this time continuing straight into the Thompsons Bridge area parking lot off of DE 92. Walk left on the highway to cross the creek and return all the way back to the Hidden Pond Trail. Turn right.

Follow the red blazes of the Hidden Pond Trail as it curves to the right, leaving the forest and passing by a meadow. The way reenters the forest and soon returns to the Tulip Tree Woods Nature Preserve. Gigantic trees watch over the land as it must have looked when this country was young. The Indian Springs Trail comes in from the left rear and joins your route. The two trails shortly reach a low stone wall at the edge of the woods. Turn left along the stones and you will very shortly come upon a break in the wall. Step through the opening and head left across the grassy area to the nature center parking lot.

2. Bellevue State Park

Through the forests and meadows of a former du Pont estate

Hiking distance: 2.25 miles
Hiking time: 1 hour
Maps: USGS Marcus Hook and Wilmington North;
park map

The names du Pont and Delaware have been linked inextricably since 1802 when Eleuthère Irénée du Pont built his black-powder mill along Brandywine Creek. The mill began an enterprise that grew into one of the largest manufacturing concerns in the world. The du Pont family has played active roles in Delaware's industrial, commercial, social, and political circles from that time to the present. For example, Delaware owes many of its museums and its great collections of decorative arts to the philanthropy of the du Ponts. The walk described here also must be counted among the gifts of the du Ponts because it winds around Bellevue, one of the former great estates of the family. Since 1976, when Bellevue became a state park, the forests, fields, and landscaped gardens of the estate have been open to the public.

The Bellevue manor house was constructed in the 1850s by Hanson Robinson, a wealthy sea merchant, at a cost of $100,000. William du Pont Sr., grandson of Eleuthère Irénée, purchased the estate in 1893 and added to it over the years. The present appearance of the mansion and the grounds is largely due to the efforts of William du Pont Jr., who inherited Bellevue in 1928. He was a dedicated tennis and horse enthusiast and developed a virtually unequaled indoor-outdoor recreational and sporting facility on the estate. William Jr.'s second wife, Margaret Osborne du Pont, was a tennis champion who won five French, seven Wimbledon,

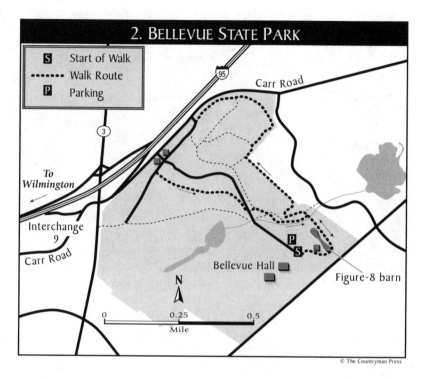

2. BELLEVUE STATE PARK

S	Start of Walk
••••••	Walk Route
P	Parking

95

Carr Road

3

To
Wilmington

Interchange
9

Carr Road

N

Bellevue Hall

Figure-8 barn

0   0.25   0.5
Mile

© The Countryman Press

and an unprecedented twenty-five U.S. national titles in singles, doubles, and mixed doubles from 1941 to 1962. Trials for tennis tournaments at Forest Hills and Wimbledon were held here, and in 1943 Bellevue hosted the National Women's Tennis Championships.

The horse facilities at Bellevue especially catch the attention of today's visitors. A 1.125-mile racetrack, an indoor figure-eight riding arena, an indoor galloping track, steeplechase schooling fences, individual stables complete with paddocks, an extensive layout of additional stables, and a horseshoe-shaped formal garden filled with topiary shrubbery depicting riding paraphernalia illustrate William Jr.'s love of horses and equestrian sports.

As you might guess, most visitors come to Bellevue State Park to play tennis or ride horses. In addition, an extensive network of bicycle trails is

Once the home of William du Pont, Jr., Bellevue is now a state park open to all.

widely used, including a portion of the Northern Delaware Greenway Trail. The park is also a good place for walking. Some of the wooded back areas of Bellevue are well worth exploring on foot, especially during the spring wildflower display. The park contains small but significant remnants of old-growth woodlands, an increasingly rare ecosystem in the Piedmont.

The walk I recommend follows bicycle paths and bridle trails into a less-developed portion of the 328-acre park. Towering black oak, red oak, tulip tree, and sweet gum approach 120 feet in height. The herbaceous ground layer brightens in the spring with jack-in-the-pulpit, trout lily, May apple, spring beauty, wild geranium, toothworts, and violets. In the fields and meadows, common dandelion, white mustard, and field garlic grow in stands among the grasses.

Most of the horse trails at Bellevue are covered with cinders or wood chips; thus, the hiker usually is spared the churned-up mud that horses' hooves can create. Ticks are found in the fields, so check yourself carefully after the hike.

Access

Bellevue State Park is located on the northeastern perimeter of Wilmington. From downtown, go north 3.9 miles on I-95 to interchange 9, labeled "Delaware 3—Marsh Road." The exit ramp leads you to Carr Road. Turn left (north) here and continue on Carr Road across Marsh Road. At 0.4 mile from the intersection with Marsh Road, turn right into the park. An entrance fee is charged from May 1 to October 31. Drive for 0.7 mile to the last parking lot, following the signs to the tennis courts.

Trail

From the big parking area, walk up the short stairway toward the tennis courts. Bellevue has the only public clay courts in the state. The building on the left, the cabana, is today the tennis pro shop, but it used to serve as a dressing room for guests when the swimming pool was here. Turn left (east) on the paved bicycle path that runs between the parking lot and the tennis courts. The path leads around the large, figure-eight barn. The barn was moved here from Pennsylvania by William Jr. for indoor equestrian events. The barn and the attached hunter barn now are used for large gatherings and meetings and as an indoor picnic facility.

The paved path circles the barn and connects with the Northern Delaware Greenway Trail. Continue straight into the woods in a north-westerly direction, crossing a small stream on a bridge. Just beyond the stream a paved trail enters from the right and the paved Northern Delaware Greenway Trail veers sharply to the left. You will return to this spot later, but for now continue straight on a broad, dirt trail, going slightly uphill.

Your wide trail angles left where a narrow path goes right. Soon you will see another side trail leading right. Follow it uphill. At the top of the rise, the path turns left into an old, grand avenue lined with sycamores and maples.

Reach a large meadow with scattered spruces and woody shrubs at the end of the lane. Turn right immediately, following a path through the grasses at the edge of the woods. Your trail soon enters the forest, part of

Bellevue Woods Nature Preserve, and descends gradually to a small stream. Near the creek, jog right and cross an old stone wall at the base of a gigantic tulip tree. Continue following the trail downstream until it turns left and crosses the creek on a wooden bridge.

Once over the bridge, the trail ascends gradually and leaves the woods. At the meadow, a trail leads off to your left front, but keep straight on a single track that leads through the field. The way curves gradually left to parallel Carr Road on the right. The trail leaves the meadow and Bellevue Woods Nature Preserve and enters a mowed, landscaped area. The park has placed nesting boxes for eastern bluebirds on posts along the meadow margin. Follow the worn, single track through the grass. An asphalt trail joins from the right rear and the way is now paved as it goes along the edge of the park entrance road.

Take the right fork at a split in the trail. Cross the entrance road and walk along the grassy shoulder. The buildings on the right were once gatehouses for the estate and were relocated here when I-95 was built. One of the buildings is now the park office and nature store. Continue straight across the driveway and walk on a double track leading through a small grove of trees.

You soon reach a paved road and cross it diagonally. Your wide trail enters a forest of tall trees and thick undergrowth. The way comes close to a paved trail just outside the woods on the right, but the tracks remain separate.

Continue straight on a mowed, grassy path when you come upon an intersecting trail at the edge of the forest. Your trail curves left to cross the park entrance road. Once across the road, you are walking on a paved trail again. Go about 100 feet and turn right on a paved trail. Almost immediately, the asphalted Northern Delaware Greenway Trail comes in from the right. Continue straight at a cross trail and soon return to the trail junction encountered earlier in the hike. Turn right and retrace your steps to the parking lot and your car.

Two other of William Jr.'s vast holdings in Maryland are also open to the public. His Fair Hill estate for racehorses and fox hunting is now Fair Hill Natural Resources Management Area (see the next hike), and the Reinecke Fuchs Farm, his exclusive preserve on the Choptank River, is now the Jean Ellen du Pont Shehan Audubon Center and Sanctuary.

3. FAIR HILL NRMA

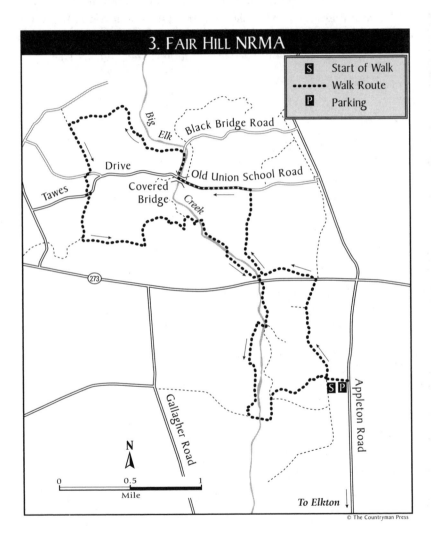

S	Start of Walk
••••	Walk Route
P	Parking

Big Elk

Black Bridge Road

Drive

Old Union School Road

Tawes

Covered Bridge

Creek

273

Appleton Road

S P

Gallagher Road

N

0   0.5   1
Mile

To Elkton

© The Countryman Press

3. Fair Hill Natural Resources Management Area

Crisscrossing Big Elk Creek

Hiking distance: 8.25 miles
Hiking time: 4 hours
Maps: USGS Newark West; natural resources management area map

Fair Hill was the Maryland country estate of William du Pont Jr., the wealthy Delaware banker and financier who also owned Bellevue Hall near Wilmington (see the previous hike in Bellevue State Park). He began acquiring land in Maryland in 1926 to ride to hounds. The hunt, known as Foxcatcher Hounds, was the first step in making Fair Hill an outstanding equestrian center. Within a decade, William Jr. had added a racetrack and barns for his thoroughbreds. Here he stabled racehorses under the sapphire-blue silks of his Foxcatcher Farm.

The Great Depression gave William Jr. an opportunity to buy adjoining lands. He capitalized on his enormous wealth and seemingly boundless energy to mold Fair Hill into his own remarkable vision of what a horse farm should be. He continued to buy and trade land to consolidate Foxcatcher Farm into one large, contiguous property. By the mid-1950s, Fair Hill covered more than 7,600 acres in northern Maryland and neighboring Pennsylvania. It was one of the largest private landholdings in the East.

William Jr. hunted at least three times a week before breakfast and then went to his bank in Wilmington. Sportswriter Red Smith described him as a "thin-shanked millionaire who rides like a border raider, and works like a longshoreman."

The Foxcatcher Farm covered bridge cost $1,165 to build in 1860. The span crosses Big Elk Creek in Fair Hill Natural Resources Management Area.

He died in 1965. His heirs sold about 2,000 acres of the Pennsylvania portion of Fair Hill to private interests, but the Maryland holdings (more than 5,600 acres) were bought by the state of Maryland in 1975 to be used as a park.

Hikers and other outdoor devotees, including horseback riders and mountain bikers, are the lucky recipients of Maryland's foresight. An estimated 80 miles of trails wind through what is today the Fair Hill Natural Resources Management Area. Many of the routes are the same as those used during the du Pont years. Fox chasing and horseracing continue to attract equestrian enthusiasts today. The trails are shared by hikers, bikers, and riders. They traverse a picturesque rolling countryside of deciduous forests, grassy meadows, stream valleys, wetlands, and ponds. More than half the area is mantled in mature woodlands. Through the middle runs south-flowing Big Elk Creek.

This hike uses some unmarked paths and parts of three of the natural resource management area's five color-coded loop trails to explore some of the best places. These color-coded trails, totaling about 21 miles, are the main stems from which the other, unmarked trails branch. Use this walk as an introduction to this superb area. You can plan later hikes by consulting the excellent trail map for sale at the natural resources management area office on Tawes Drive.

Fair Hill is closed to hikers and other visitors during the deer shotgun management hunt, usually for two days in early January. Call the area office at 410-398-1246 if you are planning to walk during that time.

Access

From downtown Elkton, drive north on MD 268 for 0.9 mile to its northern terminus at MD 279. Turn right (north) onto MD 279 to cross Big Elk Creek and then turn left (north) onto MD 316. Follow MD 316 for 2.6 miles to its northern terminus at MD 277. Continue straight at this intersection, driving north on Appleton Road. Stay on Appleton Road for 2.2 miles to a gravel parking area for Fair Hill Natural Resources Management Area on the left. The parking areas at Fair Hill require a fee using self-service pay boxes.

Trail

Follow the double track west from the back of the parking lot. The way passes through a gate in the "super fence"—a chain-link and concrete barrier under construction at the time of William Jr.'s death to keep foxes from escaping. It was never finished. Just beyond the fence, intersect with the Yellow Trail going straight and to the right and another, unmarked trail going left. You will return to this spot later from the front, but for now turn right (north) and walk along the fencerow on a double track.

The route is marked with yellow blazes on trees and posts. After passing through a woodlot sheltering a small stream, the Yellow Trail climbs and turns left in a meadow. Continue straight on an unmarked double track, leaving the Yellow Trail behind for now.

Cross MD 273 on a bridge. Immediately on the other side, reach the Green Trail that goes straight and to the left. Turn left, paralleling the state route and descending gradually on an old highway with broken pavement.

Pass under a trail bridge and shortly you will reach the bottom of the hill. Ahead is a bridge across Big Elk Creek. You will cross the creek bridge later in the hike, but for now stay on the Green Trail by turning right and beginning a steady ascent that lasts for about the next half mile.

Reach a T-intersection with Old Union School Road; here you and the Green Trail turn left. The road, which is used only by park vehicles, passes by a fieldstone house with some associated outbuildings before it reaches Big Elk Creek. The Green Trail turns right to proceed upstream, but your route continues straight for the first crossing of the creek on a covered bridge. The span, built in 1860, is named Foxcatcher Farm Bridge from when William Jr. owned the land. On the other side of the bridge the paved road continuing straight is Tawes Drive and the gravel road to the right, leading upstream along the creek, is Black Bridge Road. A large parking lot is at the corner. The big stone house visible ahead, sitting on a terrace above the creek, was designed and built by William Jr. in 1944–45 as a hunting lodge. It now is the Fair Hill Nature and Environmental Center. Turn right on the Orange Trail, which follows Black Bridge Road and Big Elk Creek north (upstream) a short distance.

Pass a picnic pavilion on the left. Just before reaching a bridge over the creek, make a sharp, hairpin turn to the left rear onto a dirt service road that intersects with Black Bridge Road. Walk uphill on the service road for just a few feet and then turn right on a path through the woods. The trail into the woods is marked with orange blazes on trees.

The way climbs through a beautiful forest on the steep ridge above the creek. The narrow path is densely canopied for about the next mile. Follow the orange blazes, at one point descending steeply to reach a cross trail where you turn left, and eventually reach a vehicular double track. Turn left again.

Follow the vehicle track to an unpaved road and turn right, uphill. The Orange Trail leaves the road after about 500 feet by turning left into the woods, still climbing.

After a short distance, the Orange Trail descends to paved Tawes Drive, jogs left on it to cross a run, and then turns right on a path. These turns are well marked with orange blazes.

The trail climbs to a high meadow where the tall grasses seem always to wave in the breeze even on the hottest summer days. The elevation here is about 340 feet, the highest point along today's hike. The path skirts the meadow, at times leading along a hedgerow of Osage orange. Beyond the meadow, the Orange Trail divides, with the way to the right leading in 0.75 mile to the trailhead parking lot on MD 273. Turn left to continue on the Orange Trail loop.

The path goes through forest for about the next 0.75 mile. Follow the orange blazes as the route drops into a ravine with a pretty little stream and crosses the Nature Trail several times. In each case, the Orange Trail continues straight while the Nature Trail entwines to either the left or right. After the Nature Trail and stream, the Orange Trail climbs steeply to reach a hilltop meadow. It follows the curving edge between the meadow and the forest and then turns sharply left to leave the meadow. The way goes downhill rather steeply through the woods.

At the bottom of the descent, the Orange Trail levels and curves to the left. Turn right onto a wide, mowed, unmarked side trail, leaving the Orange Trail behind. This will be the first side trail you encounter after leaving the hilltop meadow. Your way curves right and drops into the bottomland of Big Elk Creek. You are walking downstream on the right bank. You may not be able to see the water because of the plant growth, but you can hear it off to your left. Keep right at a fork and you will soon reach a side trail to the left that leads in just a few feet to a bridge across the creek.

Once on the left bank, turn right and follow the creek downstream through a lush bottom of grasses, wildflowers, and tall trees. The creek is often out of sight behind a wall of chaotic plants, but you can hear the water gurgling and bubbling in its stony bed.

Reach a side trail to the right that leads to another bridge. Back on the right bank, turn left and continue making your way downstream. The route here is straight and narrow, following a lane between a sloping, private pasture on the right and the creek's riparian forest on the left. Your trail curves left to cross the creek on an old highway bridge that was built in the mid-1930s. The bridge leads to a spot near the Green Trail that you encountered earlier. Turn right and continue downstream on a double track.

Go under MD 273. The way continues to its junction with the Yellow Trail, which comes in from the left and runs straight ahead along the creek bank. Turn right on the Yellow Trail as it crosses the creek on a bridge. Back on the right bank, follow the yellow blazes as you climb out of the floodplain on a curving path. The Yellow Trail passes through a stunning upland forest on the ridge above the creek. The trees are younger and scrubbier just before the trail leaves the forest and enters a meadow. In the middle of the meadow, the Yellow Trail intersects a double track and turns left toward the creek.

Cross Big Elk Creek for the sixth and final time on the Scott's Mill Bridge. On the left bank you will see the remains of Scott's Mill, a three-story-high fieldstone structure that is being overtaken by the forest. After the ruin, you come to a T-intersection, where you turn left, staying on the Yellow Trail. Continue straight where a double track goes to the right. Just beyond a crossing of a run on a concrete slab bridge, the Yellow Trail turns right and climbs out of the Big Elk Creek valley on a single track.

The route passes through a spectacular forest of tall red oak, white oak, beech, and tulip tree. It reaches the intersection where the spur trail leads straight through the "super fence" to return to the parking lot on Appleton Road.

4. White Clay Creek State Park

A circuit hike through a park rich in scenery and history

Hiking distance: 5.75 miles
Hiking time: 3 hours
Maps: USGS Newark West; park map

L ying hard against the Pennsylvania border, this Piedmont park pre-serves about 3,400 acres of gently rolling, picturesque hills. Small streams dissect the terrain and flow into White Clay Creek, a national wild and recreational river. A large, rocky upthrust tells of ancient earth movements and is one of the very few such outcroppings found in Delaware. Trees grow tall and stately in the woodlands. Wildlife is var-ied and abundant; the park is an Important Bird Area of National Sig-nificance as recognized by the American Bird Conservancy and the National Audubon Society. White-tailed deer are so common that hunt-ing is allowed.

A walk at White Clay Creek State Park can also broaden your histori-cal perspectives, since the park protects significant sites that figured prominently in local history. The first European farmers came to the White Clay valley in the mid-1700s, attracted by the rich bottomlands, abundant stone for building houses and barns, and numerous springs coming from the steep slopes. Your trail passes by an old springhouse where water still gushes forth from beneath the native stone foundation.

Boundary disputes among Delaware, Maryland, and Pennsylvania kept the status of this area in doubt for many years. The confusion arose because of inaccuracies in land surveys, mistakes that remained uncor-rected even after Charles Mason and Jeremiah Dixon were called in to

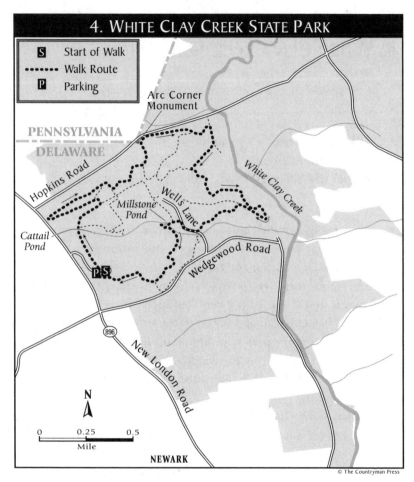

4. WHITE CLAY CREEK STATE PARK

S Start of Walk
••••• Walk Route
P Parking

Arc Corner Monument

PENNSYLVANIA
DELAWARE

Hopkins Road

White Clay Creek

Wells Lane

Millstone Pond

Cattail Pond

P S

Wedgewood Road

896

New London Road

N

0   0.25   0.5
Mile

NEWARK

© The Countryman Press

define Delaware's circular northern boundary and to establish the east-west line marking the border between Maryland and Pennsylvania and the north-south line marking the border between Maryland and Delaware. The arc was supposed to meet the east-west and north-south lines at the same point, but it missed the east-west line by almost 1 mile. The region became known as the Wedge. Bandits and other outlaws moved into the area. Using the deep woods as hideouts, they launched raids into neighboring jurisdictions, escaping into the Wedge. The area was also the scene of bloody prizefights as unscrupulous promoters from Philadelphia, sidestepping laws that banned boxing in all three states, staged matches in the disputed Wedge. A compromise that extended the Mason-Dixon Line eastward to intersect the circular boundary gave this land to Delaware in the late 19th century. Your trail passes by this point, called Arc Corner.

The rock outcrop, also on your trail, was the scene of a small, early-day quarrying operation, providing millstones for a nearby water-powered gristmill. Two incomplete millstones, partially cut out of the rock but never used in the old mill, remain behind.

White Clay Creek State Park is a favorite destination for hikers. A trail network consisting of over 30 miles of footpaths includes named and blazed trails, a physical fitness trail, and numerous unmarked trails. Walkers can explore almost all parts of the park. You can also connect with even more trails in the adjacent Middle Run Natural Area (a New Castle County park) and Pennsylvania's White Clay Creek Preserve, which is just across the border and upstream of the Delaware parks. If far horizons beckon, head out on the long-distance Mason-Dixon Trail, 5 miles of which pass through White Clay Creek State Park. Walking west on the Mason-Dixon Trail will lead you to the Appalachian Trail in the Pennsylvania mountains; walking east will bring you to the Brandywine Trail at Chadds Ford, Pennsylvania. The hike featured here links several different trails, including part of the Mason-Dixon Trail, to lead through the woods and fields on the west side of White Clay Creek.

The state park is divided into four sections. Your walk is in the Carpenter Recreation Area, named for Walter S. Carpenter Jr., honorary chairman of the board of the DuPont Company in 1975 when the firm donated about 100 acres to Delaware as an addition to the park. Subsequent donations by DuPont created the White Clay Creek Preserve in both Delaware and Pennsylvania. The Delaware portion of the preserve is another section of White Clay Creek State Park. The park, preserve, and

A rough-hewn and incomplete millstone of Wissahickon schist sits on the shore of Millstone Pond in White Clay Creek State Park.

the Middle Run Natural Area protect almost the entire upper White Clay Creek watershed.

Some hiking trails are closed to all but hunters during shotgun deer season (generally on selected days of November, December, and January). Hunting is never permitted on Sundays in Delaware. Telephone the park at 302-368-6900 if you have questions.

Access

White Clay Creek State Park is on the northern edge of Newark. From downtown, drive north on DE 896 for 2.7 miles. Turn right into the park and continue for 0.2 mile to the large parking area. An entrance fee is charged from May 1 to October 31. Your trail begins on a lane blocked by a vehicle gate on the left side of the parking lot.

Trail

Head down the broad lane, which serves as the route for three separate trails: the yellow-blazed Twin Valley Trail, the blue-blazed Millstone Trail, and the red-blazed Life Course Trail. Scholastic cross-country runners also race in the park, so you will see trail signs labeled x-c. The Millstone Trail soon turns right at a hedgerow, but you keep straight on the Twin Valley and Life Course Trails.

Walk through the park's disc golf course in an old field. A short side trail in a vale leads right to Cattail Pond, a little impoundment that is the headwaters for a stream you will see later in the hike.

Follow the leftmost trail as you ascend out of the vale (the way on the right is part of the disc golf course). The Life Course Trail goes right, but you continue straight on the Twin Valley Trail. The way curves right at the top of the rise, staying in the old field. The field is overgrown with wild roses, Japanese honeysuckle, Virginia creeper, blackberries, and multitudinous young trees. The fragrant roses and honeysuckles are in bloom in late May and early June. Many birds and small mammals make their homes in this thicket.

The Twin Valley Trail turns sharply left, leaving the old field and entering the woods. It immediately curves left again and then turns right, but here you continue straight on a wide unnamed trail. After some twists and bends, the way comes close to DE 896 and curves right in a broad U-turn, leaving the highway behind. The trail is a wide, mowed swath through hedgerows, old fields, and scrubby woods near the northern boundary of the park. You pass along the edges of a white pine plantation and a bamboo grove.

Rejoin the Twin Valley Trail by continuing straight where it comes in from the right. The yellow-blazed trail dips and climbs and then tunnels through a dark grove of fir. Pass by an abandoned house surrounded by an overgrown clearing. At a T-junction with a broad trail, turn left and go downhill.

You will come to another T-junction, this one with the Mason-Dixon Trail, marked with blue paint blazes on trees and posts. Turn left and continue your descent; you are now walking on the combined Mason-Dixon and Twin Valley Trails. The 190-mile-long Mason-Dixon Trail traverses some of the eastern lands traveled by Mason and Dixon in their famous land survey of 1763–67.

The wide trail descends more steeply and passes an old springhouse on the right. Continue downhill, paralleling the little run fed by the spring, and come upon a small meadow. Your trail turns right here to cross the branch on a wooden bridge. Visible a few feet ahead in the clearing is a stone obelisk about 5 feet high—the monument marking Arc Corner and Delaware's border with Pennsylvania. Bearing the date 1892 and the names of commissioners from both states, the stone is the easternmost marker along the Mason-Dixon Line. (The western end is more than 250 miles from here, near the Ohio River.) Arching northeastward from this point is the circular boundary between Delaware and Pennsylvania, drawn using the Court House spire in New Castle as the center of the 12-mile radius (see chapter 8). The road on the far side of the meadow is Hopkins Road.

To continue, follow the trail across the branch and reenter the woods. The way narrows to a single-file footpath and passes through a dense grove of large white pines, climbing gradually to a T-junction. The Twin Valley Trail goes right, but you turn left and stay on the Mason-Dixon Trail.

Descend steeply on the narrow path and reach a T-junction with the wide Tri-Valley Trail in the White Clay Creek bottomland. The Mason-Dixon Trail turns left at this junction, but you go right on the Tri-Valley Trail.

Immediately after crossing a small stream on a bridge, turn right off the Tri-Valley Trail onto an unnamed trail. Climb along the side of the ravine, keeping the stream on your right. The way passes through a mature forest of beech and white oak and bestows pleasing vistas of little falls and water-splashed boulders.

You arrive at a T-junction with the combined Mason-Dixon and Twin Valley Trails after about 0.25 mile. Turn left and continue walking uphill, although the way is now less steep. Your path enters a second-growth forest, characterized mostly by young tulip trees, and curves right in a hairpin turn.

Next your trail turns left and descends slightly, narrowing as it enters a mature forest to cross a hillside high above a little stream on the left. Old beech trees dominate this lush, south-facing slope. The stream arises from Cattail Pond, which you saw early in the hike, feeds into Millstone Pond, which you will soon reach, and flows into White Clay Creek.

You come out onto paved Wells Lane. Turn right and follow the road uphill. (The Mason-Dixon and Twin Valley Trails turn left on the road and cross the little stream.)

After passing a house on the left, turn left off the road onto a wide unnamed trail that borders an old field. A side trail descends from the right through the field to intersect your trail, followed very shortly by another trail coming in from the right. Turn onto the second trail, climb slightly, and reach the earthen dam impounding Millstone Pond.

The small pond is surrounded by aquatic vegetation and home to water snakes, frogs, fish, and myriad insects. It evidently served as a millpond in years past, because the rocky upthrust overlooking the water has two unfinished millstones partially cut from the surrounding rock— one at the pond's edge and the other on the outcrop. The bedrock is hard Wissahickon schist with seams of gneiss—ideal for making millstones for grinding grain. Embedded in the rock are chips of shiny mica and orange-colored feldspar, along with larger veins of whitish quartz. Turn left and walk across the grass-covered dam to reach the Millstone Trail at a T-junction at the base of the outcrop. Turn left and descend. At the bottom of the dam, cross a wide trail and keep straight, following the blue blazes of the Millstone Trail.

The route follows a broad, mowed swath through a young forest, although a few individual trees are much older and larger. Reach a small stream and begin an ascent up the little valley, eventually crossing the run before climbing steeply on steps to reach higher ground. The trail leads through a particularly scenic part of the park as it crosses little side ravines on wooden bridges. After an unnamed trail goes right, the Twin Valley Trail comes in from the left and joins the Millstone Trail. The two trails run together from this juncture to where they return to the starting trailhead.

Your path crosses the small stream for the second time very near its headwaters.

Very shortly afterward, the way leaves the forest and enters a large grassy meadow. Turn right and walk uphill along the edge of the woods to a hedgerow, where you turn left. Woodchucks are common in this area because they like to dig their burrows a few feet inside the forest at the edges of meadows and fields. Follow the hedgerow to the end and then angle right to climb to the trailhead.

5. Elk Neck State Forest

A circuit hike around the Plum Creek watershed

Hiking distance: 6.25 miles
Hiking time: 3 hours
Maps: USGS North East; forest map

The sandy, well-drained soils of Elk Neck—a large, wedge-shaped peninsula near the head of the Chesapeake Bay—dictate the types of plant and animal communities that live there. The dry uplands support slow-growing, stunted trees. In the past, frequent fires had further depleted the soils and resulted in even poorer quality tree growth. In an effort to conserve the environment, prevent wildfires, and demonstrate modern forestry practices, the state of Maryland began acquiring parcels on Elk Neck in the mid-1930s. Today's result is the 3,465-acre Elk Neck State Forest.

The state protects the young trees in their fragile, upland habitats and also preserves many fine stands of larger trees on the lower slopes and along the streams. The bottomlands, by and large, have escaped the influence of fires. The forest needs protection from wanton abuse because mining interests, attracted by the sand and the large, underlying deposits of accompanying gravel, have opened several nearby quarries. The state forest is a reserve where tree scientists experiment with hybrid species to improve timber growth and where hikers and other visitors can explore the woodlands. Elk Neck is a good place to practice your skills in identifying animal tracks; the soft, sandy soils along the trail provide a clear record of the passage of many forest animals. The tunnels of eastern mole are also often seen, although the subterranean animals themselves are elusive.

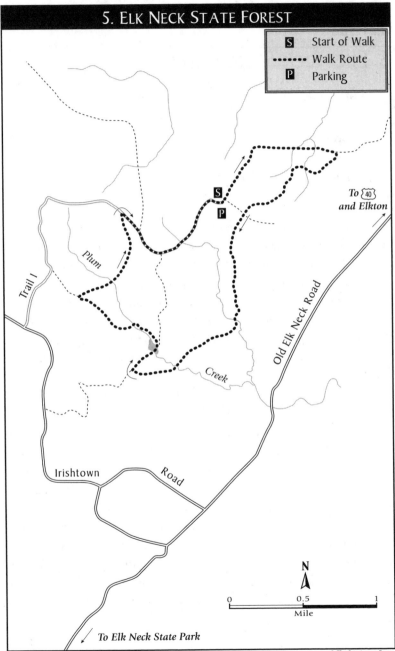

5. ELK NECK STATE FOREST

S Start of Walk
•••••• Walk Route
P Parking

*To 40
and Elkton*

Plum

Trail 1

Old Elk Neck Road

Creek

Irishtown   Road

N

0   0.5   1
Mile

↙ *To Elk Neck State Park*

© The Countryman Press

The hike featured here circles the Plum Creek watershed and also crosses some upland areas where drier forests can be observed. About half the hike is on the Mason-Dixon Trail. This 190-mile footpath crosses the northern portion of Elk Neck in its course between the Appalachian Trail in the Pennsylvania mountains and the Brandywine Trail along Brandywine Creek in the Pennsylvania Piedmont. The Mason-Dixon Trail, named for the surveyors who helped settle the boundary dispute among Pennsylvania, Maryland, and Delaware, passes through all three states.

Please keep in mind the following safety tips as you hike on Elk Neck. The forest is used by hunters during legal open seasons in their quest for white-tailed deer, squirrels, eastern cottontail, northern bobwhite, and mourning dove. Use common sense during hunting season and wear protectively colored clothing. Maryland prohibits hunting on Sundays on state land. Call the forest office at 410-287-5675 to plan your hike. Ticks and mosquitoes may be found along the brushy sections of the path, so bring repellent. About a mile of your walk follows a gravel road through the forest; vehicular traffic is usually light.

The route I recommend is but one of a number of hikes that can be enjoyed on the foot trails, hunter access trails, firebreaks, and gravel roads weaving through the forest. You will see a couple of former primitive campsites that are closed pending a management review. Use this hike as an introduction to Elk Neck and then explore further on your own, using the excellent trail map available for sale at Elk Neck State Park.

Access

From Elkton, go west on US 40 for 1.8 miles and then turn left (south) onto Old Elk Neck Road. Drive for 3.9 miles to Irishtown Road and turn right (northwest). After 2.3 miles, the main entrance to Elk Neck State Forest appears on the right. Turn and proceed along a gravel road (called Trail 1) for 2.5 miles. You will arrive at a split in the road where both forks are gated. There is room to park several cars along the road, but be careful not to block access to either gate.

Trail

Begin your hike on the left fork (a continuation of Trail 1). Walk around the vehicle gate and go along the wide, gravel road. Eventually you will cross two small streams in rather quick succession. They are carried under the road by culverts and are the headwater arms of a creek that flows north. After the second crossing, climb slightly. As the road levels, be alert for a trail that comes in from the right—the Mason-Dixon Trail, marked here on trees and posts with bicolored paint blazes (blue on the top and white on the bottom). The distinctive blaze is used on Maryland state lands to avoid confusion by hunters with the dark-blue paint stripe landowners may place on their boundary trees to post their property as NO TRESSPASSING. Turn right on the Mason–Dixon Trail, leaving the wide road and walking on a narrow path through a semimature forest of sweet gum, sassafras, beech, red maple, scrub pine, and scarlet, white, willow, and chestnut oak.

The dense undergrowth on either side of the trail consists of blueberries, grapes, mountain laurel, and occasional American chestnut shoots growing from old stumps. Chestnut once dominated dry woods from Maine to Illinois and south to Georgia and Mississippi, accounting for between one-third to three-fourths of all the hardwoods in eastern forests. They are now represented only by small sprouts springing from the insistent roots. Attacked by a fungal disease imported accidentally from Asia at the turn of the 20th century, virtually every American chestnut tree died in less than 40 years. The collapse was an ecological disaster of immense magnitude. Now, 100 years after the epidemic spread through the forests, the chestnuts of Elk Neck and elsewhere in the East are still struggling against total extinction. Sprouts along the trail stand 6 to 7 feet tall and flower in June; a few may even produce nuts in the autumn. The shoots may live about 20 years and reach 15 feet or so before their bark shatters from the fungus and the tree becomes girdled and dies.

Cross Trail 3 (a gravel road closed to traffic) and continue straight around a vehicle gate. The path widens as it skirts the forest boundary on the left.

Shadows play across a wet meadow created when a dam on Plum Creek ruptured and drained a pond in Elk Neck State Forest.

You begin a wide circle around a flooded bottomland as the trail turns left and narrows. The path curves to the right and descends to cross a stream on a wooden bridge. The way curves left again and soon approaches Plum Creek. Beavers had flooded the path at the time of my last visit. Mason-Dixon Trail maintainers have temporarily moved the trail downstream of the dam so hikers can cross on a wooden bridge or wade the gravelly creek at low water.

Beyond the creek, climb gradually for 0.75 mile on a broad path, coming out onto Trail 2, a gravel road closed to traffic. Turn right, downhill. The Mason-Dixon Trail here joins a completed stretch of the Elk Neck Trail, a footpath marked with white, lighthouse-shaped blazes on trees and posts. It is under construction by the Elk Neck Trails Association. When finished, the trail will extend about 12 miles along the length of the Elk Neck peninsula and connect Elk Neck State Forest with Elk Neck State Park.

Near the bottom of the hill, a research plantation on the left marks one of the foresters' efforts to improve timber production on Elk Neck by planting hybrid trees (loblolly pine crossed with pitch pine). The Elk Neck Trail turns left into the research plantation at an old picnic ground to circle around the upper shore of the former Plum Creek Pond. You will rejoin the Elk Neck Trail later, but for now continue straight on the Mason-Dixon Trail to cross a ruptured dam on Plum Creek. Scramble down and up the breach, wading the creek at the bottom. (Plans call for removing the rest of the dam and spanning the creek with a bridge.) The old Plum Creek Pond (on the left) is a wet meadow where, in the summer, dragonflies constantly patrol the flats and hawk mosquitoes and other small insects.

The Mason-Dixon Trail stays on Trail 2 to the end of the guardrails and then turns left (west) to get around the wet meadow. You come again to the Elk Neck Trail, here at its current northern terminus after looping around the old pond. The Elk Neck Trail may be relocated in this area to extend it even farther north. Stay on the westbound Mason-Dixon Trail, which shares its route with the southbound Elk Neck Trail for a short distance.

Turn left and cross Plum Creek on a wooden bridge. Shortly beyond the span, the Elk Neck Trail currently continues straight, on its way around the old pond to its southern end at the Turkey Point Lighthouse. You turn right, staying on the Mason-Dixon Trail. Your path skirts a big lowland on the left, then drifts away from the bottom and turns right. The way gradually descends and crosses Plum Creek for the fourth and final time.

Come out onto graveled Trail 1 and turn right, staying on the Mason-Dixon Trail. The trail soon turns left to reenter the woods, but you continue straight on the road. From here it is almost 1 mile to your car. You will pass the former Barred Owl Nest campsite on the right, Trail 2 on the right, and the old Fox Den campsite on the left.

6. Elk Neck State Park

Upland forests surrounding a tidal marsh and a beach

Hiking distance: 4.25 miles
Hiking time: 2 hours
Maps: USGS Earleville; park map

Elk Neck State Park was established in 1936 when outdoor recreational areas were being developed by the Civilian Conservation Corps (CCC). The CCC was a New Deal emergency relief program designed to combat the unemployment of the Great Depression and to restore lands that were ruined and blighted by generations of abuse. President Franklin D. Roosevelt wrote and signed an organizational plan for the CCC on his first day in office in 1933. He noted at the bottom, "I want personally to check the location, scope etc. of the camps, size, work to be done, etc.—FDR."

Within three months of Roosevelt's declaration, a thousand camps were in operation and more than three hundred thousand young men were at work in forests and parks. The trails, roads, picnic areas, and cabins constructed under the CCC program at Elk Neck State Park are still enjoyed by visitors today. Largely because of the CCC effort, Elk Neck features five different hiking trails (including a nature trail) totaling over 9 miles.

The land stewardship tradition continues with the Maryland Conservation Corps (MCC). Created in 1984 by the Maryland General Assembly in an attempt to improve environmental conditions in and around the Chesapeake Bay, the MCC is a public service program focused on state lands and natural resource conservation. MCC crews now work around the state, not just near the bay. The program changes slightly from year to year, but a normal year for an MCC worker starts in October and lasts for ten and a half months. The typical participant is a college graduate in her or his early twen-

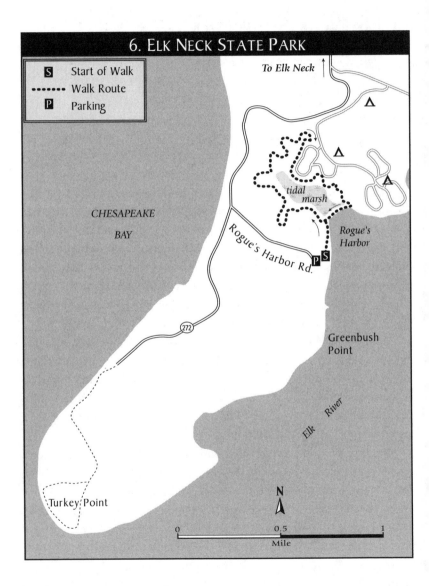

6. ELK NECK STATE PARK

S Start of Walk
••••••• Walk Route
P Parking

To Elk Neck

CHESAPEAKE

BAY

tidal marsh

Rogue's Harbor Rd.

Rogue's Harbor

P S

272

Greenbush Point

Elk River

N

Turkey Point

0   0.5   1
Mile

ties who may be looking to improve specific labor skills, who wants to serve her or his country, who has an interest in conservation, land management, or environmental science, and who likes to spend time outdoors. Workers come from all over the country. Crews are trained for tasks such as trail maintenance, ecological restoration, fire management, chain saw operation, and visitor services.

The Maryland Park Service manages the MCC crews with funding from AmeriCorps and the National Recreation Trail program. Proceeds from the sale of Elk Neck State Park trail maps funnel into the MCC, so be sure to purchase one of the excellent trail maps that show all the trails at Elk Neck State Park and Elk Neck State Forest. They are available at the park office and camp store.

The MCC has built new observation decks, benches, and bridges along several of the old CCC trails. The paths enable hikers to explore the varied topography of the park, ranging from high bluffs and sandy beaches along the Elk River and the Chesapeake Bay to marshlands surrounded by mature upland forests.

Wildlife is abundant because of the environmental diversity. Big birds such as bald eagle, wild turkey, and great black-backed gull are found here, along with many kinds of songbirds and waterfowl. White-tailed deer, beaver, eastern gray squirrel, and eastern box turtle abound.

Most of this hike traverses the Orange Trail, the longest in the park, so-called because it is marked with orange paint blazes on posts and tree trunks. You may find some old blazes of different colors from when a part of this route was called the Black Trail, but the way is easy to follow. The big parking lot at the Rogue's Harbor Boating Facility is the best trailhead for day hikers, but campers at the park campground can easily reach the Orange Trail from either the Susquehanna or Wye loops. The hike is best done during low tide. Higher tides can squeeze the Rogue's Harbor beach and fill the channels that connect the marsh to the harbor. Tide information can be obtained from the park office, the camp store, or the boat store at the Rogue's Harbor Boating Facility.

Lush forests in Elk Neck State Park are among the many attractions of this peninsula on a peninsula.

Access

From Elkton, go west on US 40 for 1.8 miles and then turn left (south) onto Old Elk Neck Road. Drive 8.3 miles to a T-junction with Elk River Lane in the hamlet of Elk Neck. There, turn right, and then left (south) again immediately at a stop sign onto MD 272. After 2.1 miles, you will enter Elk Neck State Park. Proceed for 2 more miles and turn left onto Rogue's Harbor Road, which leads to the Rogue's Harbor Boating Facility. An entrance fee is charged for using the boating facility, but hikers without boats may be able to park free. If the road to the boating facility is closed, you can park on the right shoulder opposite the entrance and walk to the trailhead. When past the entrance booth, drive an additional 0.4 mile to a large parking lot on the left. Park your vehicle near the far left middle of the lot, away from the sailboat masting area.

Trail

At the far left middle of the parking lot, behind a line of boulders, head down a wide, grassy trail that descends gradually. The way is bordered with small trees, mostly sweet gum. A ditch lined with riprap begins on your left. After about 500 feet, you will come upon the Orange Trail, going to the left and also going straight ahead down to a beach on the Elk River. You will return to this spot late in the hike, but for now turn left and cross the ditch on a wooden bridge. Immediately the Orange Trail curves right where a faint, white-blazed connecting trail comes in from the left.

The path is thickly surrounded by blueberry. The tidal marsh the Orange Trail encircles is visible through the trees on the right. Reach an observation deck, placed for good views of a large beaver lodge located near the shore. Beaver have been living in the marsh and using the lodge for decades. Signs of tree cutting by these rodents are evident near the trail and in the lowland. Arrowheads, yellow iris, and other aquatic plants can be seen in the shallows. Park rangers have placed nesting boxes for wood duck on wooden posts throughout the marsh. Each post is collared by an inverted metal cone fitted beneath the boxes to keep out marauding raccoons and other predators. The effort has paid off because the marsh is a favored place to observe wood ducks. In May, mother ducks followed by broods of tiny ducklings can be seen paddling and diving about the aquatic vegetation.

The path descends and ascends in turn through lowlands where little runs flow into the tidal wetlands. These rich bottomlands are carpeted with ferns with imaginative and lyrical names: sensitive, cinnamon, lady, and marsh.

Your trail eventually reaches the ridge above the head of the marsh, where excellent views reach across the entire wetlands to the beach on Rogue's Harbor and the Elk beyond. The way then descends into a broad, ferny lowland laced by a small creek feeding the marsh. Cross the watercourse on a wooden bridge and soon climb a long, steep bank into an upland forest. Tulip tree, American holly, mountain laurel, oaks, beech, flowering dogwood, tall pawpaw, and sweet gum are some of the trees and shrubs bordering the path.

The Orange Trail curves right where a white-blazed connecting trail goes left and an obscure path continues straight. The paint blazes are somewhat confusing at this junction; take care to turn right and soon you will find orange blazes confirming that you are on the correct path. A little beyond, the Orange Trail splits, with a left arm going out to Campground Access Road and the narrow, main trail continuing straight. Both routes are marked with orange blazes; go straight to continue your hike.

The trail skirts around the Wye Loop of the park campground. There is a junction with a white-blazed cross trail that leads right to the marsh edge and left to the back of campsite 51. The Orange Trail comes out briefly onto the paved road near campsite 68 in the Susquehanna Loop to get around a deep ravine but then returns to the woods.

The Orange Trail curves sharply right and descends as a white-blazed connecting trail joins from the left. The side trail leads up and comes out opposite campsite 65 in the Susquehanna Loop. The Orange Trail passes through a fine stand of tall pawpaw near the bottom of the hill and reaches the tidal flats along the Elk River. An informal fisherman's path forks right to the beach, but your trail stays left on a less well-defined path that is mostly overgrown by rank vegetation. It very soon intersects a white-blazed connecting trail that continues straight along the river. At this junction, your trail makes a sharp, hairpin curve to the right to reach the beach.

The beach is a curving, sandy bar separating the marsh from Rogue's Harbor, a cove of the broad Elk. A short stream flows from the marsh, across the bar, and into the cove near where the trail comes into the open. The stream can be easily leaped when the tide is out. If you are here at high tide, be prepared to wade or to go upstream where the water breaks out of the reeds; there you may be able to scramble across on piles of driftwood.

Walk along the crescent-shaped beach. I have seen everything from bald eagles to big ocean freighters during visits here. The eagles patrol the shallow waters near shore for fish and the ships are far out in the

river sailing to or from the Chesapeake & Delaware Canal. Eastern kingbird and tree and bank swallows are abundant in the warmer months,
busily catching insects on the wing. Scattered about your feet are picturesque samples of driftwood and multitudinous shells of wedge rangia, a
brackish-water clam at the northern limit of its range. Waves off the shallow cove usually break gently on the shore; it is a welcome place to pull
off your boots and socks and go wading—or even swimming.

When you are ready to continue hiking, proceed to the other end of
the beach, cross another small channel from the marsh, climb a bank of
riprap, and turn left to ascend a gradual, graveled incline. You soon arrive
at the spot where you first picked up the Orange Trail. Retrace your steps
along the short spur to the parking lot.

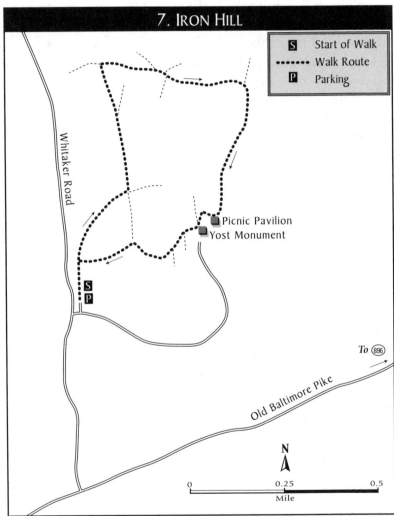

7. IRON HILL

S Start of Walk
•••••• Walk Route
P Parking

Whitaker Road

Picnic Pavilion
Yost Monument

To (896)

Old Baltimore Pike

N

0   0.25   0.5
Mile

© The Countryman Press

7. Iron Hill

An enigmatic hill rich in geological, archaeological, and historical lore

Hiking distance: 2 miles
Hiking time: 1 hour
Map: USGS Newark West

When walking the slopes of Iron Hill, you follow the ancient footsteps of indigenous peoples who came here to mine jasper for their stone tools and weapons. You will also cross the paths of 18th- and 19th-century miners who opened small, primitive shafts and pits in the hillside to extract iron ore. When near the summit, you can imagine how American rebels used the hill during the Revolution to spy on British troop movements.

The story of Iron Hill begins in a distant geological age. Its origins are dim and not fully understood by scientists. Today, it is a strikingly prominent topographic feature, visible from afar. Iron Hill, together with Chestnut Hill, its slightly lower neighbor to the northwest, forms an island of gabbro (a granular, igneous rock) surrounded by the sandy sediments of the Coastal Plain. It is the highest point south of the Piedmont on the Delmarva Peninsula. The hill's summit stretches to 320 feet above sea level, but it appears higher, especially when viewed from the east, where its hulking, steep slopes tower 270 feet above the surrounding plain.

Early man was attracted to the hill, perhaps for spiritual reasons due to its unusual features and certainly because of the presence of jasper. Archaeological studies show that prehistoric Indians conducted a rather sizable quarrying operation on the southwest flank of the hill, chipping out jasper blocks with stone tools of gabbro and then fashioning the jasper into projectile points, knives, choppers, scrapers, drills, and other flaked implements.

The ancient native quarries were largely obliterated in the 1700s and 1800s by white settlers looking for another mineral they regarded more highly than jasper. Welshmen from Pennsylvania, aware of the reputed reserves of iron ore on the hill, opened the first, small mine shafts after being granted this tract of land by William Penn in 1701. The highland became known as Iron Hill, the name still used, and for about the next two hundred years miners broke out chunks of iron ore with sledgehammers and picks, loaded it into cable cars and wagons, and carried it to small furnaces where it was converted into steel tools and weapons.

Mining was not continuous during this period but flourished or waned depending upon economic conditions. Some of the last open pits were operated by George F. Whitaker from 1862 to 1884. The discovery and exploitation of richer iron deposits in the Midwest, coupled with the development of the modern blast furnace, caused the demise of small, marginal mines like those on Iron Hill. The final workings were in 1891. Today, the mining scars are softened by large trees and other vegetation, but you can still discover weathered remnants of iron ore in the old pits pocketing the hillside.

Iron Hill also played a small role in the American Revolution. In August 1777, a party led by General George Washington, including Major General Nathanael Greene and the Marquis de Lafayette, rode to the crest of the hill to reconnoiter British troop movements. The British were planning to mount an attack against Philadelphia, the metropolis of English America and the rebel capital, by sailing up the Chesapeake Bay, disembarking their troops near the head of the bay, and then marching quickly into Pennsylvania to capture the city. Washington and his men sighted only a few enemy tents along the Elk River in Maryland before a severe summer storm forced them from the summit and into a nearby farmhouse where they sought shelter for the night. The storm was an ominous beginning to a bleak period for the American cause. Philadelphia fell to the British the following month, and Washington

Stella the trail dog pauses at the monument to Robert V. Yost on the Mason-Dixon Trail near the summit of Iron Hill.

moved the Continental Army into a watchful encampment at Valley Forge for the winter.

This loop hike is in Iron Hill Park, a 335-acre unit of the New Castle County Department of Parks and Recreation. The trail begins near the base of the hill, follows a circuitous route through the woods to a picnic area near the summit, and then descends to the starting point. A short stretch of the hike is on the Mason-Dixon Trail, a long-distance footpath that weaves along the borderlands of Delaware, Maryland, and Pennsylvania.

Access

From the center of Newark, go south 3.2 miles on DE 896. Iron Hill comes into view on the right as you pass through Newark's southern outskirts and cross the Christina River and I-95 (the Delaware Turnpike). South of I-95, DE 896 runs along the eastern flank of the hill. At the first intersection beyond I-95, turn right (southwest) onto Old Baltimore Pike, which follows the former post road, established in 1666, that connected Baltimore with Philadelphia. In 0.9 mile, pass the Iron Hill Museum on the right. Continue for 0.1 mile farther and turn right (north) onto Whitaker Road. The road takes its name from Whitaker, the miner, who worked on the hill in the late 1800s. Proceed 0.4 mile and turn right into Iron Hill Park. A small parking area is seen immediately on the right. Just beyond, turn left into a drive leading to a larger parking lot and leave your car.

Trail

At the end of the lot, go around a vehicle barricade and walk uphill on a broad, gravel service road. In about 300 feet, a side trail descends from the right. This path will be your return loop; for now, keep straight on the service road, still climbing uphill.

After about 0.25 mile, you reach a cross trail. Turn left off the service road onto a broad, dirt path. The way leads shortly to an extensive bank of old mine tailings on the right. The mound is covered with large trees and Christmas ferns. The forest throughout this section has seemingly experienced relatively little disturbance in recent years. Oaks, hickories, tulip tree, and beech tower to great heights with comparatively little understory. Beyond the mound of mine tailings, the trail narrows slightly. About 0.25 mile from the service road, the woodland trail forks at the head of a small ravine. Take the left fork and walk downhill, following the side of the ravine and keeping it on your right.

The trail curves away from the ravine as it continues downhill. Come upon a T-junction and turn right. The sound of vehicular traffic from I-95 can be heard in this area. Your trail soon angles left and joins with the blue-blazed Mason-Dixon Trail as it comes uphill from the left. Continue straight at this juncture and soon you will see on the right high piles of tree-covered rock and dirt that mark the old iron mines. Some mounds are 30 feet high. This is a good place to look for rusty red, pitted rocks of iron ore on the trail and on the steep mounds.

Just beyond the piles of mine tailings you will come upon a multiple junction of woodland paths. Use caution here in selecting the correct trail.

First, angle slightly right, avoiding the broad trail to the left that descends steeply. Immediately thereafter, the trail forks, with both forks going uphill. The Mason-Dixon Trail continues on the right prong, but your choice is to take the left fork. After a few steps, a cross trail is encountered; turn left onto it and continue along a more or less level forest path in an easterly direction.

Proceed for about 0.25 mile to a T-junction. Turn right and climb steadily to near the summit of Iron Hill. Keep straight when you encounter side trails and you will reach the border of the county park. Private homes are visible to the left. Turn sharply to the right and soon you will see the end of a high, chain-link fence on your left. Continue straight past the fence end and past a side trail to the right. Turn left at the first opportunity onto a side trail.

The land drops off steeply on the right side of the trail as you walk along the top of the old mine diggings, some of which are water-filled. The trail then curves to the left, away from the pits, and comes out of the woods at the Iron Hill Pavilion; the picnic shelter sits on the west face of the hill, slightly below the crest. Turn right on the paved path and descend to the summit parking area.

Walk along the head of the parking lot and cross the Mason-Dixon Trail. A marble monument to Robert V. Yost, the founder of the Mason-Dixon Trail, is at the trail junction. Keep straight on the walkway that leads into a small picnic area and follow the paved, curving path to where it ends at the back left corner. There you will pick up a broad, dirt trail that leads into the forest.

You will very soon reach a T-junction. Turn right. Continue straight on the wide trail past two narrow side trails that come in from the left. When you reach a third trail to the left, take it and follow this path downhill to where it intersects the service road on which you began this hike. Turn left and descend to your parked vehicle.

8. Old New Castle Historic District

A stroll through Delaware's colonial capital

Hiking distance: 1.25 to 4.25 miles, depending on side trail
Hiking time: 1 hour plus
Map: USGS Wilmington South

M any small cities and towns of Delaware and the Eastern Shore have historic districts, open spaces, and unique flavors well worth discovering on foot. New Castle, Delaware, is a prime example. It is an authentic colonial town, complete with 18th-century homes still inhabited, some cobblestone streets that have not been asphalted, an ancient church or two with well-kept graveyards, a workable town plan from the 1600s that has been lovingly and proudly preserved, and public buildings associated with the early patriots of our country. The piquant fragrance of two-hundred-year-old boxwood hovers along the shady side streets. To add even further to its appeal, New Castle is a place largely undiscovered by tourists.

New Castle owes its present-day appearance mainly to the happenstances of history. The town served as the English colonial capital of Delaware from 1704 to 1776. When the Revolutionary War broke out, New Castle became the capital of the new state of Delaware. The fledgling government was forced to flee inland to Dover in 1777 when British warships on the Delaware River captured John McKinly (the "President of Delaware State") and threatened the town. With the fall of Philadelphia and with the British armada in full control of the Delaware River, New Castle was isolated. The state government never returned. After the war, New Castle regained some of its prominence by serving as a trade center

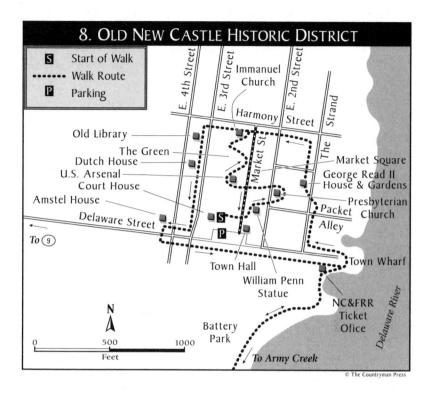

8. OLD NEW CASTLE HISTORIC DISTRICT

S Start of Walk
•••••• Walk Route
P Parking

E. 4th Street
E. 3rd Street
E. 2nd Street
Immanuel Church
Harmony Street
Market St
The Strand

Old Library
The Green
Dutch House
U.S. Arsenal
Court House
Amstel House
Delaware Street
To ⑨

Market Square
George Read II House & Gardens
Presbyterian Church
Packet Alley

Town Hall
William Penn Statue
Town Wharf

N

0   500   1000
Feet

Battery Park

NC&FRR Ticket Ofice

Delaware River

To Army Creek

© The Countryman Press

and as the county seat of New Castle County. The city largely escaped the menace of human negligence and uncontrolled urban expansion of the 19th century. By the late 1800s, New Castle had been eclipsed by burgeoning Wilmington to the north, and the county government moved to the larger city in 1881. Left on the sidelines again, New Castle missed the urban upheavals of rapid growth that characterized the first part of the 20th century. Thus, the downtown area of today's New Castle looks much as it did in early times. There are automobiles, utility poles, and other modern accoutrements, but I suspect that many figures from the 1700s would still recognize New Castle if they could visit the town today. The historic district is a Registered National Historic Landmark.

New Castle traces its beginning to 1651, when Dutch colonists built Fort Casimir on the site. The Dutch settlement was an effort to counter Swedish excursions into territory Holland claimed in the early 1600s as a result of Henry Hudson's exploration of the Delaware River. In 1654, Swedes from Fort Christina (today's Wilmington) captured Fort Casimir and renamed it Fort Trefaldighet ("Trinity," so called because the tiny post fell to Sweden on Trinity Sunday).

The Dutch returned in force the following year, recaptured the fort, and named it New Amstel. They turned New Amstel into a bastion, the southern outpost of New Netherlands in North America. Peter Stuyvesant, director-general of New Netherlands and headquartered in New Amsterdam (today's New York), came to New Amstel and laid out the town streets and The Green (the central marketplace) in 1655. Dutch rule was short-lived, however, for in 1664 England captured all of Holland's holdings in North America; after overpowering Stuyvesant's colony of New Amsterdam, Sir Robert Carr led the expedition against New Amstel. The settlement was placed under the rule of the Duke of York (later King James II) and became New Castle. The Dutch regained control briefly in 1673–74 during the Third Anglo-Dutch War, but New Castle was returned to the English by the Treaty of Westminster in 1674 in exchange for British islands in the Pacific.

New Castle remained British for over 100 years, so most of the heritage seen by today's visitor is English. In 1682, William Penn arrived in the New World at New Castle and took possession of the vast land grant given to him by the Duke of York. In addition to what became known as Pennsylvania, New Castle itself was specifically deeded to Penn, along with surrounding land extending to a 12-mile circular boundary. Penn's rule proved capable, and New Castle prospered despite disputes with Lord Baltimore in neighboring Maryland. Friction eventually developed as well with Penn's central colony, Pennsylvania, and Delaware demanded its own home government. Penn reluctantly agreed and granted a separate assembly to the Three Lower Counties On Delaware in 1704. Delaware was born and New Castle was named the capital.

Your walk begins at the Court House, weaves through the heart of the historic district, and includes a spur through a riverside park. The museums and historic houses along the way that are open to the public have varied hours. Most are closed during the winter months and on Monday and holidays throughout the year. Some charge a small admission fee.

To plan your trip, write or telephone the New Castle Visitor Bureau, P.O. Box 465, New Castle, DE 19720, 1-800-758-1550, or log onto www .visit newcastle.com.

Access

New Castle can be reached by DE 9, 141, or 273. Once in town, drive southeast along Delaware Street to the historic district and park your car near the Court House.

Trail

Begin at the old Court House, with the flags of the Netherlands, Sweden, Great Britain, and the United States flying from the front balcony. Originally built in 1732, it has been restored to its 1804 appearance based on a drawing by Benjamin Henry Latrobe.

Charles Mason and Jeremiah Dixon, in their surveys of 1763–67 in which they recalculated Penn's original land grant, used the spire atop the cupola of the Court House as the center of the 12-mile-radius circle that forms Delaware's northern boundary with Pennsylvania. That line, extending westward, became famous for dividing the slave states of the South (including Delaware) from the free states of the North (including Pennsylvania). See chapter 4, White Clay Creek State Park, to hike the trail that goes by the point where the 12-mile radius intersects the east-west Mason-Dixon Line.

In 1775, the colonial assembly, meeting in this building, appointed delegates to the Continental Congress. News of the signing of the Declaration of Independence was read from the balcony on July 4, 1776. Afterward, units of the Kent County militia and the Delaware Regiment ransacked the building of all symbols of the English crown and burned them in the

Built in 1707, the Presbyterian Church is the oldest house of worship in New Castle.

street. The new state assembly met here from 1776 to 1777 and drafted the first Constitution of Delaware. The building is now managed by the Delaware Division of Historical and Cultural Affairs as the New Castle Court House Museum. Admission is free and guided tours are available. Free maps of the historic district can be obtained here, too. Although a museum, the Court House is still a working building—the New Castle County Court meets here occasionally.

Back outside, turn left on Delaware Street and cross Market Street to the Town Hall, built in 1823. The City Council meets in the second-story chamber. The arch and two rooms on the first floor were designed as a fire station. Walk through the arch into Market Square, used as a market as early as 1682, the year William Penn arrived in town. The statue of Penn in the square shows him holding the gifts given to him by the Duke of York—"turf and twig and water and soyl." The land transfer was complete when the symbolic materials exchanged hands during the feudal ceremony known as the livery of seizin.

Walk across East Second Street to the Presbyterian Church. Built by the English in 1707, it absorbed an earlier Dutch Reformed Church that dates to 1657. Graves of early worshippers are scattered around the foundation and about the churchyard. Unmarked, cracked tombstones in the burial ground are from the Dutch era; several marked graves are from the pre-Revolutionary period. The church is open to visitors and worshippers.

Walk back across East Second Street, Market Square, and cobbled Market Street. Note the curbstones on Market Street. They are flat, rectangular-shaped stones, quarried from along the Susquehanna River in the early 1800s, with two holes drilled neatly into them. The holes held spikes that supported the tracks of the New Castle & Frenchtown Railroad. The railroad failed a few years after starting operations in the 1830s. When the track was torn out, New Castle residents salvaged the sleeper stones and put them to use for all sorts of purposes.

Once across Market Street, you enter The Green, or Market Plaine. The Green was designed by Stuyvesant to serve as a common ground for the townspeople to graze their livestock and as a center for "great fairs and weekly markets."

The long, two-story brick building on The Green, facing Market Street and Square, was built by the federal government in 1809 to serve as the U.S. Arsenal in preparation for a possible confrontation with England. In 1831, troops from nearby Fort Delaware on Pea Patch Island were garrisoned here temporarily after their fort was destroyed (see chapter 9). After the Mexican War (1848), the building served as a school and later as a restaurant.

Past the old Arsenal, at the end of The Green, enter the cemetery of Immanuel Church by walking through a gate. The graveyard contains the tombs of many early statesmen, including that of George Read, one of three New Castle men who signed the Declaration of Independence. The church itself, with its landmark clock tower, was rebuilt in 1982 after a disastrous fire gutted the interior in 1980. When it was founded in 1689, it was the first Church of England parish in Delaware. Episcopalian today, Immanuel Church is open to visitors and worshippers.

Exit the graveyard through the Market Street gate, turn left, walk to the end of the block, and turn left on Harmony Street. Go to the next intersection (East Third Street), cross it, and turn left on the rising-and-falling brick sidewalk. The octagonal Old Library (1892) houses a museum operated by the New Castle Historical Society. Admission is free.

Most of the other buildings on East Third Street facing the Green date from the late 18th or early 19th century. The newest is the Rodney House (built in 1830 and still a private residence) at the corner of East Third Street and Silsbee Alley. The oldest is the wooden-roofed Dutch House, another holding of the New Castle Historical Society and open to the public as a museum (an admission fee is charged). Despite its name, the house was probably built around 1700, well after Dutch colonial rule ended. Historians note that both Dutch and English building traditions can be seen in the house's construction.

Turn right on Delaware Street, go to the next block, cross East Fourth Street, and arrive at Amstel House (1738), another museum of the New Castle Historical Society (an admission fee is charged). The house's main claim to fame is a wedding reception in 1784 with George Washington in attendance. New Castle justice James Booth wrote, "The Great Man stood upon the hearthstone and kissed the pretty girls—as was his wont."

Walk across Delaware Street, turn left, and go all the way to the Delaware River. At the end of the street in Battery Park on the right stands the original ticket office of the New Castle & Frenchtown Railroad (NC & FRR; 1832), with a re-created section of wooden track on a foundation of sleeper stones. The train replaced an earlier stage line that ran to Frenchtown, Maryland, on the Elk River, an arm of the Chesapeake Bay. New Castle was once an important rail center, serving passengers as they shuttled from boats on the Delaware and the Elk. The 17-mile NC&FRR roughly followed the same route as the Chesapeake & Delaware (C & D) Canal, completed in 1829. It was the first railroad in Delaware and ran one of the first steam-powered passenger trains in America. The first steam locomotive on the tracks, the English-built *New Castle*, rolled along at speeds of up to 10 miles per hour—that is, when it ran. The wooden rails rested on the individual stone sleepers; there were no crossties to connect the two tracks. The passage of heavy locomotives and cars caused the tracks to spread apart, resulting in frequent derailments. Maybe that is why the NC&FRR lost the economic battle to the C&D Canal, which still operates to this day (see chapter 11).

You can extend your walk by 3 miles by following the paved Battery Park Trail along the river through Battery Park. Traditionally, The Battery was the site of cannon emplacements of the early 1700s designed to protect the town from pirate attacks. Benches, picnic tables, and a playground are features of the park. The Battery Park Trail extends downriver to Army Creek. Sweeping vistas stretch across the Delaware River to the New Jersey shore, while close-up views of plants and wildlife are afforded by Gambacorta Marsh on the other side of the path. The trail is an excellent place to practice your birding skills by listening for the clearly different calls of the two species of crows found on Delmarva. American crow, with its familiar, loud *caw*, is almost invariably found in the trees and shrubs of the city on the landward side of the trail. The slightly smaller fish crow, which frequents the shoreline and wharves of the river on the other side of the trail, utters a short, nasal *car*. There are places along the path where you can hear a stereophonic rendition of the calls of both crows at the same time.

Walk as far as you wish on the Battery Park Trail and then return the same way to the foot of Delaware Street, site of the town wharf in the days when New Castle was a maritime center and one of the most important ports of entry in North America. William Penn stepped ashore here in October 1682, with 100 Quakers on the 300-ton ship *Welcome*. If you examine the piles of boulders and riprap lining the river, you will discover more stone sleepers from the old railroad.

With your back to the river, walk up the right side of Delaware Street and turn right at the first street—The Strand. Named after a fashionable London avenue, The Strand was the bustling waterfront street of the busy port, lined with inns, taverns, ship chandler's shops, and offices. These old buildings have been converted into private homes, and today The Strand is shady and quiet. The third alley on the right is Packet Alley, so-called because a wharf at the end of the little street received packet boats with passengers from Boston, New York City, and Philadelphia, who transferred here to stagecoach or train and continued on to Baltimore, Washington, or southward by way of the Chesapeake Bay.

Farther along, on the left, is the George Read II House (1801), a remarkably fine example of Georgian architecture. The meticulously restored house is managed by the Historical Society of Delaware and is open to the public (an admission fee is charged). Entrance also gains access to the 2.5-acre formal garden that was created in 1847—the oldest existing garden in Delaware.

Continue along The Strand to Harmony Street, turn left, walk to Market Street, and turn left to return to the Court House.

9. Pea Patch Island

Boat excursion and hiking on an island in the Delaware River

Hiking distance: 2 miles
Hiking time: 1 hour plus
Maps: USGS Delaware City; park map

This short walk features an outstanding natural area and a 19th-century fort. The setting is 161-acre Pea Patch Island in the middle of the Delaware, America's widest river. The entire island is preserved as Fort Delaware State Park. Pea Patch is named after a colonial-era tale of a boat loaded with peas that ran aground on a shoal. The spilled peas sprouted in the rich mud.

A 90-acre stand of small trees and shrubs in the northern part of Pea Patch is a specially managed nature preserve. The grove is separated from the rest of the island by a strip of marshland and serves as the nesting area for thousands of wading birds. A list of superlatives shows how important the rookery is to the region's ecosystem: It is the largest rookery in Delaware, the largest Atlantic Coast nesting ground north of Florida for wading birds, and the largest rookery of mixed species on the East Coast. Between 10,000 and 24,000 birds use the site annually. Just about every wading bird listed for the Delaware Basin comes here to build nests and raise its young: great blue heron, little blue heron, tricolored heron, black-crowned and yellow-crowned night herons, glossy ibis, great egret, snowy egret, and cattle egret. The island is the only known place in the state where black-crowned night herons nest. They, along with yellow-crowned night herons, are listed as endangered in Delaware. The rookery houses the largest breeding population of cattle egrets in the entire Middle Atlantic region. Pea Patch Island has been designated an Important Bird

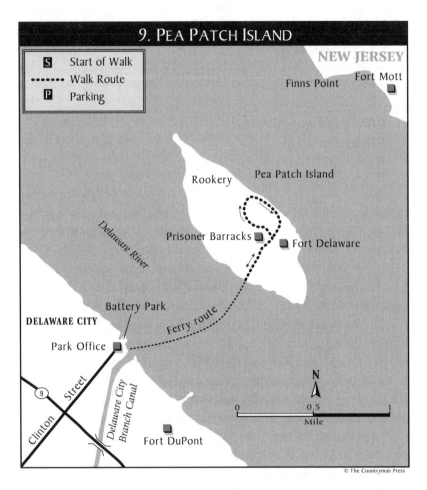

9. PEA PATCH ISLAND

Symbol	Legend
S	Start of Walk
••••••	Walk Route
P	Parking

NEW JERSEY

Finns Point   Fort Mott

Rookery   Pea Patch Island

Prisoner Barracks   Fort Delaware

Delaware River

Battery Park

Ferry route

DELAWARE CITY

Park Office

9   Street

Clinton

Delaware City Branch Canal

Fort DuPont

N

0   0.5   1
Mile

© The Countryman Press

Area by the American Bird Conservancy and the National Audubon Society in recognition of its continent-wide role in providing essential habitat for breeding birds.

Entry to the rookery itself is by permit only, for the birds are easily disturbed by human intruders. A low viewing tower on the trail enables hikers to see the colony from across the marsh. During nesting season (generally from mid-March to mid-July), the tangled branches and heavy underbrush are alive with the long-legged waders. Be sure to bring your binoculars.

The high ground on the southern part of Pea Patch is the site of Fort Delaware, a granite bastion that was designed to protect the sea approaches to the upriver ports of New Castle, Wilmington, and Philadelphia. The first fortification on the island was a star-shaped fort built in 1823. It was one of a series of coastal forts placed at strategic locations in the first half of the 19th century to defend Atlantic seaports. Pea Patch Island, lying in the center of the broad Delaware, was considered a key to the defense of the river. Military planners linked the range of the fort's guns with sister batteries on the mainland—Fort DuPont on the Delaware shore and Fort Mott on the New Jersey side.

The first Fort Delaware was destroyed by fire in 1831. The post's soldiers were transferred to the U.S. Arsenal in New Castle (see the previous hike), and the Army applied for appropriations to replace the island fort. In 1847, Congress budgeted $1 million to construct the largest modern coastal defense installation in the nation, surpassing even Fort Sumter in size. The big, five-sided stone fort, still standing today, was built in the 1850s and was garrisoned at the outbreak of the Civil War.

Typically, institutions such as military posts, prisons, mental hospitals, and universities are sources of both income and concern for local residents. Fort Delaware was no exception. The post never came under attack during its long history, so the men stationed there often had time on their hands between their regular, often boring, soldierly duties. Elijah Brooks, editor in the early 1800s of the Salem *Messenger* across the river in New Jersey, referred to troops at the nearby garrison as "desperadoes from that den of iniquity, Fort Delaware."

The post entered its most famous (some say notorious) era during the Civil War, when it served as a prison for Southern sympathizers and Confederate prisoners of war. In April 1862, Fort Delaware received its first POWs—358 Confederate soldiers captured during the battle of Kernstown, Virginia. They were joined by thousands more during the next three years. The mainland civilians' concerns reached new levels because of fear the prisoners would break out, join northern Copperheads, and seize control of the river and its cities. In reality, the Confederates were in no shape to carry out such a plan. Twelve thousand of them were jammed into damp cells on the marshy, mosquito-ridden island. Conditions were deplorable and disease was rampant. No more than a handful of the prisoners were able to perform their duties at any given time. W. Weir Mitchell, a Philadelphia surgeon who visited the fort in 1863, wrote in his diary that "the living [had] more life upon them than in them." Of the more than 2,500 Southerners who died at the fort, most were buried across the Delaware at Finns Point, New Jersey, now a national cemetery.

After the Civil War the fort remained operational, although at a much reduced level. In the 1890s, the Army began a major overhaul to update the fort's defenses, including the installation of large "disappearing" guns mounted in concrete emplacements. The southern half of the fort was covered to accommodate these huge pieces of artillery, designed to swing down out of sight while being loaded. The defensive outpost was again fully garrisoned in anticipation of the Spanish-American War. By World War II the entire fort, even the disappearing guns, had become obsolete. In 1945, the post was decommissioned; it was acquired by the state of Delaware about three years later.

Dogs are not allowed on Pea Patch Island. The mosquitoes that plagued guards and prisoners alike are still plentiful, however; repellent is recommended.

Access

The Delaware River and Bay Authority operates the Three Forts Ferry Crossing to Pea Patch Island from the Fort Delaware State Park office in Delaware City. The office and dock are at the foot of Clinton Street, near Battery Park. The ferry, the *Delafort*, also carries visitors to Fort Mott State Park in New Jersey. The ferry runs in a continuous loop between Delaware City, Fort Delaware, and Fort Mott. Fort Delaware State Park is open week-

Like the prow of a massive ship, the granite sides of nineteenth-century Fort Delaware rise 32 feet above their reflection in a glassy moat. The fort is itself an island on Pea Patch Island.

ends and holidays from late April through September and Wednesday through Sunday from mid-June until Labor Day. The park is closed on Monday and Tuesday unless a national holiday falls on one of those days. There are no private docking facilities on the island. The *Delafort* departs Delaware City every hour on the hour from 10 to 5. Call the park at 302-834-7941 to check on current schedules. A fare is charged for passage (discounted for children ages 2–12), but no additional fees are collected for entry to the park.

Trail

Because of the mud flats encircling the island, the *Delafort* docks at the end of a long wharf. On the landward end of the wharf, a free jitney meets the boat to carry visitors to the front gate of Fort Delaware. Of course, you could also walk. The way leads for about 0.3 mile through a brackish marsh characterized by common reed, cattail, knotweed, and groundsel tree.

Your trail, the Prison Camp Trail, has numbered stations along the way to explain the history behind Fort Delaware's years as a POW cantonment. A booklet keyed to the numbered posts is for sale at the Sutler Store inside the fort.

Walk north from the moated fort's drawbridge, across the open area. The reconstructed Prisoner Barracks are visible on the left. Enter the woods on the Prison Camp Trail. Built by the Youth Conservation Corps, this wide footpath meanders through a bottomland hardwood forest of black walnut, red maple, box elder, buttonbush, black cherry, sassafras, and sumac. A few red cedar are also seen. The distant sound of a navigational horn on the Delaware mingles with the calls of thrushes and gray catbirds.

You will soon reach the wooden platform that allows you to view the heronry across the marsh. With binoculars, the large nests, often with a couple of downy young in them, are plainly visible. Adults fly about constantly or call loudly from their perches.

To continue, follow the interpretive trail as it passes a small bunker dating from the last modernization project of the fort during the late 1890s and early 1900s. The path skirts marshland and passes a rock-strewn beach, affording magnificent views across the broad river to the New Jersey shore. Binoculars will help you pick out the low profile of Fort Mott, with Finns Point just to the north. The beach here and even this trail may be submerged during very high tides or floods.

Come out of the woods and angle right across the open space to Fort Delaware's front entrance. Take time to tour the old fort. Afterward, walk to the wharf or take the free jitney that leaves the fort about 10–15 minutes prior to ferry sailings. The *Delafort's* last departure for the mainland is at 5:15.

10. Lums Pond State Park

A circuit hike around Delaware's largest body of fresh water

Hiking distance: 7.5 to 8.5 miles, depending on side trail
Hiking time: 4.5–5 hours
Maps: USGS Saint Georges; park map

A millpond was built when Saint Georges Creek was dammed in 1735 to power a sawmill. The Lum family acquired the mill around 1809, and the pond has been known as Lums Pond ever since. It was enlarged and dredged in the 1820s to serve as a feeder pond for the lock system on the nearby Chesapeake & Delaware Canal (see the next hike). When the canal was changed to a sea level route in the 1920s, the locks were eliminated and Lums Pond lost its usefulness to maritime commerce. The 200-acre pond and the land around it were declared surplus property by the U.S. Army Corps of Engineers and sold to the state of Delaware. The state park was created in 1963 and has been developed since that time as an outdoor recreation center.

The 1,790-acre park lies in populous northern Delaware and receives heavy use on summer weekends and holidays, but it is often overlooked by hikers. One of my walks in the park was on Memorial Day weekend; the picnic areas, athletic fields, boat launching areas, and campground were crowded with people, yet I did not encounter another hiker on the trail. At places along the shore the only sounds you hear are the lapping of gentle waves and the murmuring of the breeze through the trees. Many species of mammals, birds, reptiles, amphibians, fishes, and insects abound in the pond and adjacent fields and forests. The large trees in the park serve as home to colonies of wild honeybees and as nesting sites for great horned owls. All three of the mimic thrushes found in eastern

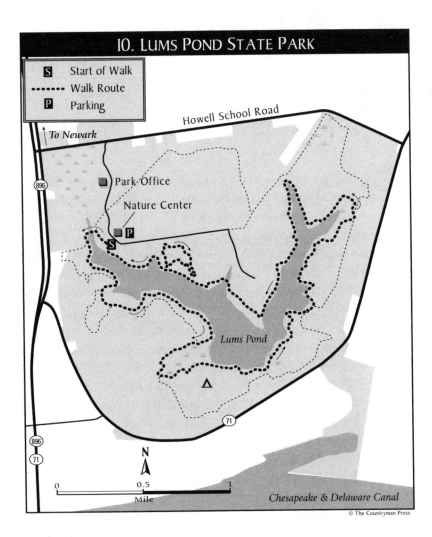

10. LUMS POND STATE PARK

S Start of Walk

•••••• Walk Route

P Parking

Howell School Road

To Newark

896

Park Office

Nature Center

P

S

Lums Pond

71

896
71

N

0   0.5   1
Mile

Chesapeake & Delaware Canal

© The Countryman Press

North America (northern mockingbird, gray catbird, and brown thrasher) are common in the park. Orchard oriole, indigo bunting, and wood thrush can be observed in the proper habitats. Black rat snake and eastern box turtle are the most frequently encountered terrestrial reptiles. Mammals likely to be spotted are eastern cottontail, woodchuck, and raccoon. Beavers are present but are rarely seen by park visitors.

If you plan to walk this trail keep in mind two important considerations. First, some trail segments are closed to hikers during shotgun deer season, usually three separate weeks in November, December, and January. Call the park office at 302-368-6989 if you are planning to hike during those months. Hunting is not allowed on Sundays in Delaware. Second, the meadows and hedgerows along the trail provide ideal habitats for ticks. Expect to encounter ticks at any season, even on mild winter days, but be especially alert in spring and early summer, when scores of ticks can be picked up in certain areas. You should check yourself carefully after you walk and remove any attached or unattached ticks. Also, be sure to inspect your youngsters and dogs.

The hike I recommend begins at the Whale Wallow Nature Center in Area 5 and follows the Swamp Forest Trail counterclockwise around the pond, with a side trip on the Life Course Trail. Access to the Swamp Forest Trail, however, can be gained at several points. For example, if you camped at Lums Pond you could easily pick up the trail from the campground.

Access

Lums Pond State Park is near Bear, 7.6 miles south of Newark. From Newark, take DE 896 south through Glasgow. Go 2.3 miles beyond Glasgow and turn left off DE 896 onto Howell School Road. The park entrance is on the right, 0.4 mile from the junction with DE 896. An entrance fee is charged from May 1 to October 31. Take the park road 0.5 mile to the Whale Wallow Nature Center parking lot on the left.

Evergreen and low to the ground, clubmosses carpet the forest floor in Lums Pond State Park. Related to ancient plants that lived 200 million years ago, they are slow-growing, taking as long as 20 years to complete their total life cycle.

Trail

To reach your trail, cross the park road and walk through a picnic area. A sign here points to the Swamp Forest Trail and a fishing pier. As you approach the pond, turn right on a wide, dirt lane—the Swamp Forest Trail.

The trail soon leaves the picnic area and turns sharply left to cross an inlet. This area is a favorite spot for fishermen, and you will likely see several anglers trying for bass, bluegill, crappie, catfish, or pickerel. The Little Jersey Trail (a multiuse trail open to hikers, cyclists, equestrians, and snowmobilers) comes in from the right to use the same crossing.

Turn sharply left again on the other side of the inlet. The trail soon forks, with the Little Jersey Trail going to the right and your path continuing to hug the shore to the left. This part of the park is largely undeveloped, enabling the hiker to enjoy long stretches of solitude. Grand vistas of quiet water framed by red birch trees appear at bends in the trail. The path stays mainly near the shore and is canopied by large oaks and beech. Beavers prowl this part of the pond; evidences of tree cutting can be seen.

The Little Jersey Trail remains close to the footpath, and on occasion the two trails share the same route, but they always return to their own orbits around the pond. When the paths diverge, choose the one to the left and you will remain on the Swamp Forest Trail close to the shoreline. The hiking trail crosses most swales and drainage ways on wooden bridges and boardwalks.

The way passes through a wet meadow filled with ferns and sedges and then climbs slightly to cross an old field. The field is filled with sun-loving wildflowers during the growing season. In just a short time, you can discover hawkweeds, clovers, hop clovers, chickweeds, speedwells, wood sorrels, asters, and goldenrods. These old fields are favorite areas for praying mantises to lay their egg cases; in late autumn and winter look for the hardened, brown, foamlike masses on stems and twigs. The eggs within the cases wait in silence for the warmer and longer spring days before hatching into young mantids.

After the third brush with the Little Jersey Trail, the path descends and crosses a deeply gullied stream on a wooden bridge, then enters a forest dominated by mature beech, hickories, and oaks. The understory is strikingly open, and spring wildflowers grow abundantly in the rich forest humus.

After about 1.5 miles, the trail turns sharply right, away from the water, to get around an extensive marsh. The pathway joins with the Little Jersey Trail again for about 0.25 mile. At one point, the two trails diverge briefly so that foot travelers can cross a stream on a bridge while riders are directed upstream to a ford. When the trails split again, the narrow footpath curves left around the lowland and the broad Little Jersey Trail stays mainly straight.

Shortly after the trail separation, your path reaches the park's campground. Turn left immediately after crossing a bridge over a gullied stream and stay on the trail in the woods. The way going straight upslope leads to campsite 45. The Swamp Forest Trail stays close to the water and skirts a fishing pier. The short pier serves not only anglers but also birders. It overlooks a quiet cove lined with tall trees. Logs extend out into the water. The trees, fallen logs, and the pier itself provide ideal perches for birds. In the warmer months, swallows are usually skimming across the water in search of flying insects. Fishing birds such as great egret, cattle egret, great blue heron, and belted kingfisher are also commonly seen here. Eastern kingbird, European starling, red-winged blackbird, and woodpeckers (especially northern flicker) are often spotted in the trees and along the shore. The logs slanting out of the water usually are crowded with basking turtles, some of them quite large. Lums Pond supports a sizable turtle population; almost any visual sweep of the water's surface will reveal turtles' heads protruding above the water as they swim along.

Beyond the campground, your trail continues for 0.25 mile to a boat launch. Cross at the lower end of the paved parking lot. The road to the right leads shortly to DE 71. After the boat launching ramp, you reenter a wild, undeveloped portion of the pond shore. The land is low and swampy here; expect muddy conditions during most of the year. Clubmosses and Christmas fern grow densely on either side of the trail. This is an excellent place to be watchful and to catch a glimpse of some of the park's more wary birds and mammals, such as American woodcock, yellow-crowned night heron, northern bobwhite, and red-tailed hawk. Where the trail approaches open fields look for woodchuck dens. Woodchucks are common in this part of the park, since they prefer to dig their burrows a few feet inside the forest at the edges of meadows and fields. These large rodents are often out during the daylight hours (except in winter) feeding on leaves and grasses.

As the trail angles easterly you cross the outlet from Lums Pond. Shortly beyond the outlet, the Swamp Forest Trail climbs a small bank and again joins the Little Jersey Trail for about 200 yards. Then the two trails split again and the hiking path reenters the woods to the left.

The trail travels through a forest of small, second-growth trees and then leaves the woods to link again with the Little Jersey Trail for the sixth and final time. The trails follow the edge of an agricultural field for about 100 feet. The footpath then crosses a hedgerow of dark, ragged Osage orange.

Rusty barbed wire can still be seen attached to some of the tree trunks, a reminder that this area used to be cropped and pastured. Descend slightly from the hedgerow through a young, brushy forest and cross an inlet on a wooden bridge. A marsh at the margin of the pond is visible on your left as you descend to the bridge.

Beyond the inlet, climb an embankment and come out of the woods onto a wide, sandy lane. To the right, the lane leads to the park's primitive youth camping area. Turn left (southwest), keeping an old field on your right and a scrubby woods on your left. Stay on the lane for about 0.5 mile as it parallels the narrow eastern arm of the pond and then turns to the right (northwest) along the northern arm of the pond. Old fields dominate this part of the park, which is set aside as a dog training area. There are a few picnic tables and campfire rings scattered around. The open land provides good opportunities to see killdeer, turkey vulture, American tree sparrow, and American crow. Cross a narrow inlet on a short dike.

Where the lane turns sharply right continue straight on a narrower, yet still broad, well-maintained path for a short distance to the head of the northern arm. There turn left sharply and cross an inlet marsh on a wooden footbridge. Turn left onto the trail at the end of the bridge and reenter the woods.

Your path stays very close to the shore here as it passes through an especially scenic area. Clubmosses form dense stands of green all the way to the water's edge. Where the northern arm enters the main body of the pond, the way turns sharply right and continues along the water. Cross a wooden bridge over a broad inlet.

After the crossing, your trail skirts a pine plantation and the park's 18-hole disc golf course. The Swamp Forest Trail keeps left and heads toward the pond, avoiding the paths leading right that are part of the disc golf course. When you reach the water's edge, turn right (a wooden fence prevents you from turning left at this point). Cross a little run on a wooden bridge. The disc golf course is upslope and on your right. When you reach a small fenced enclosure on the left, turn right. You soon reach a big grassy area and turn left. The disc golf course is now on your left in the trees.

Follow the edge of the grassy area toward the old swimming beach, now converted to a grassy sunbathing site and a wading area. As you approach the bathhouse, veer right, keeping it on your left. Just beyond the building, walk along a gravel lane that passes through the picnic area. The lane leads out of the picnic grounds to a wooden bridge crossing another of the many arms of Lums Pond. Cross the bridge and immediately turn left onto a narrow trail, keeping close to the water. Ignore the lane going straight and the path to the right.

In 0.25 mile, you reach the park boathouse, where canoes, kayaks, sailboats, rowboats, and pedal boats can be rented in the warm seasons. Turn left onto the paved path and walk toward the docks. Turn right onto the concrete quay, go to the end of the dock area, and continue on the graveled path into the woods. This area is very picturesque since the trail is close to the water's edge.

A sign on the right after 0.25 mile indicates the entrance to the Life Course Trail. Long popular in Europe, these specialized trails for building physical fitness have become increasingly common in the United States. If you want, your walking distance can be increased 1 mile by taking the fitness trail. Turn right, then keep left, following the arrows. The Life Course Trail returns to this point after 20 exercise stations set up in a pretty forest. You can walk or jog at your own pace, stopping periodically to work out at rustic equipment along the way. Signs illustrate the exercises and explain how to participate at your level of ability.

Back on the Swamp Forest Trail, cross an arched footbridge over a little inlet and immediately turn left through a grassy picnic area with a pavilion. Ignore the gravel path that goes straight. On the far side of the picnic area, a sign indicates where the trail reenters the woods. Continue along the shore to a fishing pier, where you turn right on a broad trail that leads slightly uphill. Reach a wide, dirt lane and turn left. Follow the lane to the picnic grounds in Area 5. Turn right through the picnic area and cross the road to the Whale Wallow Nature Center.

II. Chesapeake & Delaware Canal

Along a maritime avenue, still bustling after more than 175 years

Hiking distance: 7.25 miles
Hiking time: 3.5 hours
Maps: USGS Elkton and Saint Georges

The Chesapeake & Delaware Canal, or the C&D as it is called by almost everybody, is a remarkable engineering achievement that serves many purposes. First and foremost, it is a working waterway, wide and deep enough to handle large, oceangoing ships. Owned and operated by the U.S. Army Corps of Engineers, it is a crucial link in the shipping commerce of the United States. The canal shaves almost 300 miles off the water journey between Philadelphia and Baltimore and eliminates the ocean route around Cape Henlopen and Cape Charles. The passage of freighters, barges, tugs, naval ships, fishing boats, motorboats, sailboats, and yachts combined makes the C&D one of the busiest canals in the world. More than 22,000 vessels sail through in an average year, including many of foreign registry.

The canal also vitally affects the surrounding land and its people. The influence is not as great today, but in bygone days the towns and communities along the water owed their existence to the canal. Showboats and floating stores visited the wharves. Canal men and their families made up most of the townspeople. Inwardly narrow in outlook yet lying next to a great avenue of world commerce, the communities contained both provincial and cosmopolitan elements. A sense of this past can be obtained by strolling the streets of Chesapeake City, Maryland—the headquarters of canal pilots—or of Delaware City, Delaware, where the only remaining canal lock can still be seen.

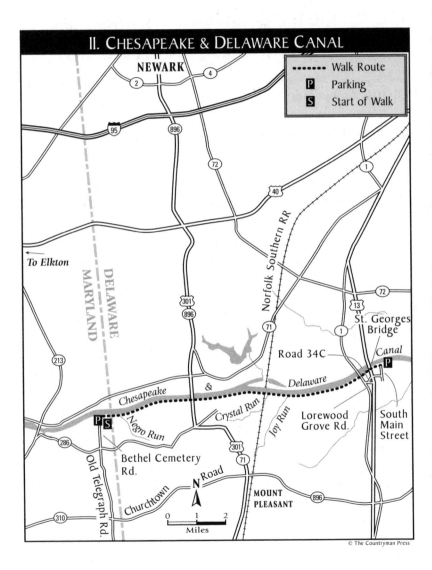

II. CHESAPEAKE & DELAWARE CANAL

······· Walk Route

P Parking

S Start of Walk

NEWARK

To Elkton

DELAWARE
MARYLAND

Norfolk Southern RR

St. Georges Bridge

Road 34C

Canal

Chesapeake & Delaware

Crystal Run

Joy Run

Negro Run

Lorewood Grove Rd.

South Main Street

Bethel Cemetery Rd.

Old Telegraph Rd.

Churchtown Road

MOUNT PLEASANT

0   1   2
Miles

© The Countryman Press

Slashing across the peninsula and creating, in effect, a large island of the southern portion of the land, the C&D has become a natural and cultural boundary between upper and lower Delmarva. (In keeping with this tradition, it is used as such in this book.) The southern portion is set apart from the mainland to the north, like another country. The region is tied more to the worlds of water and of farmland and to the customs and values that link engenders. Towns are mostly small, population densities are relatively low, and there are no interstate highways. Northern Delawareans jokingly call the southern part of their state "slower Delaware." The northern portion indeed seems more oriented to the modern, faster-paced world of the early 21st century. Lying athwart the great northeastern megalopolis, the region is crisscrossed by interstates and commercial strips. Some say even the weather changes when you cross the canal.

Augustine Herman (or Herrman or Heermans) was the first to envision a canal linking the Chesapeake Bay and the Delaware River, and he published such a proposal in 1661. He was in a unique position to assess all the possible routes this canal might take. Born in what is now the Czech Republic, a mapmaker and surveyor by trade, he was serving as the Dutch envoy from New Amsterdam to the English colony of Maryland when Lord Baltimore, proprietor of Maryland, commissioned him to make a map of the area. Herman labored for 10 years in the near-trackless wilderness, mapping not only Maryland but also what is today Delaware and much of Virginia. Lord Baltimore was so pleased with the map when it was published in 1670 that he called it "the best map that was ever Drawn of any Country Whatsoever," and he granted Herman 13,000 acres along a broad river in northeastern Maryland. Herman named the river after his fatherland, Bohemia, and called his home Bohemia Manor. From his estate he pursued his dreams of uniting the two great bodies of water—the Chesapeake Bay and the Delaware River.

First, he laid out a cart road connecting his Maryland grant with the Appoquinimink River and the town of New Castle on the Delaware River. Known as the River Road or the Old Man's Road, it may have followed part of a major Indian trail that linked the Delaware River with the upper Choptank River (see chapter 16, Martinak State Park). His canal plans, however, were never realized.

The idea of a canal resurfaced in 1788, when the youthful nation was eager to accomplish grand works. The Chesapeake & Delaware Canal Company was founded in Philadelphia, and construction of the canal began in 1804. The work halted two years later because of lack of funds. The ditch lay unfinished for 17 years before construction resumed; the canal finally opened to traffic on October 17, 1829.

Competition came swiftly three years later when the New Castle & Frenchtown Railroad began servicing roughly the same route. However, unlike the outcome in most other parts of the country where railroads won the economic battle for passenger and freight revenue, the C&D Canal Company survived and the NC&FRR failed. (See chapter 8, Old New Castle Historic District, to explore remnants of the NC&FRR.)

The federal government purchased the canal in 1919 to modernize and enlarge it for steam-powered ships. The U.S. Army Corps of Engineers was given control of the waterway. The first tasks were to eliminate the locks and deepen and widen the channel. Removing the locks did away with the need for feeder ponds, such as Lums Pond (see the previous hike), along the length of the canal. Today, the C&D is 450 feet wide, 35 feet deep, and almost 14 miles long. The eastern end enters the Delaware River at Reedy Point, and the western end empties into Back Creek at Chesapeake City, thence into the Elk River and the Chesapeake Bay. The Chesapeake & Delaware Canal is the only major commercial navigation waterway in the United States built during the early 1800s still in use.

Both banks of the canal are lined with a number of unpaved service roads. The roads near the water are passable by cars and are used by fishermen and other pleasure seekers. The roads farther up the banks are generally rougher and less frequently traveled. Side ramps connect all these routes at intervals. This hike follows the water-level route along the south bank, beginning in Maryland but soon entering Delaware. It follows the trace of the former towpath—the 19th-century course used by teams of mules and horses to pull freight and passenger barges, schooners, and

Built in 1942, the Saint Georges Bridge is the oldest of the five highway bridges across the C&D Canal. It carries US 13 on a high-level, four-lane span. The bridge replaced an earlier viaduct that was rammed and brought down by the SS Waukegan in 1939.

sloops through the canal. Other walks are possible along the north bank and along other sections of the south bank.

Few trees of appreciable size grow along the canal; walking here on sunny summer days can be hot and thirst provoking. Guard against sunburn and carry a canteen of water. Also, land bordering the C&D in Delaware is part of a public hunting area, and care should be exercised if you are hiking here during hunting season. Hunting is not allowed on Sundays in Delaware. This hike is best done with two cars to avoid retracing your route.

Access

From Elkton, drive east on US 40, entering Delaware and turning right (south) on DE 72 after 6.0 miles. Go 3.8 miles and turn right (south) onto US 13. Cross the C&D Canal on the high-level Saint Georges Bridge. On the south side, turn right at the first opportunity onto Lorewood Grove Road. Immediately turn right again onto Road 34C; you are now heading north, paralleling US 13, but the road soon circles to the right and goes under the bridge into the hamlet of South Saint Georges (2.2 miles from where you first picked up US 13). Reach a stop sign at South Main Street and turn left. Follow South Main Street 0.2 mile to where it ends at a stop sign overlooking the C&D. Turn right onto a paved street and drive close to where it intersects with the dirt service road along the canal. Park the first car along the shoulder of the paved street.

If coming from Newark, drive south on DE 72 for 9.1 miles to US 13. Turn right (south) and follow the above directions.

To reach the trailhead, drive the second car back to US 13 and turn right (south). After 3.0 miles, turn right onto DE 896. In 3.5 miles, you will come upon a major intersection in the little village of Mount Pleasant. DE 896 turns right; US 301 and DE 71 go both left and right. Continue straight (west) onto Churchtown Road, leaving the federal and state highways behind. Go through a crossroads and enter Maryland after 3.6 miles; the road becomes MD 310. Drive for only 0.1 mile and then turn right onto Old Telegraph Road. Follow this road for 2.7 miles, cross MD 286 (where the name changes from Old Telegraph Road to Bethel Cemetery Road), and arrive at Bethel Cemetery on the right just before dead-ending at the canal. Park your car along the entrance drive to the cemetery, being careful not to block access.

Trail

Walk the short distance along Bethel Cemetery Road toward the canal. A cross-shaped stone monument on the right overlooks the C&D and commemorates the Bethel Methodist Church. The 1849 church house was torn down in 1965 to widen the waterway. Turn right (east) on the dirt service road and descend to the water level. Later, side ramps will allow you either to stay near the canal or to walk along one of the upper service roads.

You will enter Delaware and the C&D Canal Wildlife Area after about 0.25 mile. Reach a wooden fishing pier slightly more than 0.5 mile from the trailhead. Anglers use the pier to capture crappie, perch, catfish, drum, and largemouth bass. In the spring, barn swallows build their nests on the beams under the pier. They usually can be seen zipping across the water in pursuit of insects. Other birds along the canal include great blue heron, black-crowned night heron, Canada goose, common merganser, northern harrier, gulls (especially ring-billed and great black-backed), fish crow, eastern kingbird, rock pigeon, and northern bobwhite. Negro Run tumbles into the canal near the fishing pier.

After about another 2 miles you will pass under the Summit Bridge. Constructed in 1960, this bridge carries US 301, DE 71, and DE 896 over the canal on a four-lane, high-level crossing; the span between the piers is 560 feet. As its name implies, Summit Bridge is near the geographic divide separating the Chesapeake and Delaware watersheds. For about the next 0.5 mile, the C&D passes through the Deep Cut; the bluff on the north bank is approximately 60 feet high and is an excellent place for fossil hunting. Most of the fossils are marine animals or their remains (such as sharks' teeth, clams, snails, and mud shrimps) dating from the Cretaceous (65–135 million years ago).

Beyond the Deep Cut, walk under the Norfolk Southern Railroad bridge, one of the longest railway lift bridges in the world. With a horizontal clearance of 548 feet, the span took four years to build. It opened in 1966. Its high towers and wide girders are preferred resting places for turkey vultures. Just east of the railroad, a culvert carries Crystal Run under the path. About 0.75 mile farther, you will see another fishing pier where Joy Run flows into the canal.

Walk another 2 miles to pass under the DE 1 bridge. This six-lane, cable stay bridge, with a main span stretching 748 feet, was constructed in 1995 at a cost of almost $57.8 million. It provides a dramatic contrast to the nearby Saint Georges Bridge, the oldest bridge across the canal (built in 1942). The houses of South Saint Georges crowd the bank as you approach the Saint Georges Bridge. Continue for about another 0.25 mile past the Saint Georges Bridge to the paved road where you parked the other car.

Chesapeake Bay

Sassafras Natural Resources Management Area

12. Sassafras Natural Resources Management Area

In a land long inhabited, imperiled species hang on

Hiking distance: 4.25 miles
Hiking time: 2.5 hours
Maps: USGS Betterton and Galena

When the state of Maryland purchased four family farms along the cliff-rimmed Sassafras River in 1995, it assumed responsibility for safeguarding four different state-listed threatened and endangered species—two plants and two animals. The big river and its shore are the key habitats for each of the rare species. One of the chief goals of the state's plan for the Sassafras Natural Resources Management Area is to make sure the critical habitats remain protected and each species thrives.

The two rare plants, both woody species, grow on the sandy beaches of the Sassafras. Sandbar willow is well adapted for life on the shifting shoals and sandbars of rivers and creeks. It grows here in small thickets on the banks along the high-tide line. The little tree, which attains a height of only about 20 feet, can be found on most rivers of central North America; it occurs as far north as Alaska and as far south as Texas. The species reaches the extreme southeastern extent of its range in northern Maryland, and here it is rare and vulnerable to riverfront alterations. Only six populations of sandbar willow are found in the state. The willows on Sassafras Natural Resources Management Area are the only ones on public land.

Beach plum is a scraggly shrub in the rose family that reaches a height of about 8 feet. It grows along the Atlantic Coast in a narrow band from

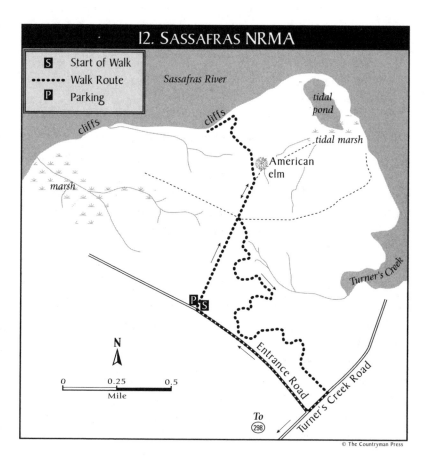

12. SASSAFRAS NRMA

S   Start of Walk
••••••   Walk Route
P   Parking

Sassafras River

cliffs

cliffs

tidal pond

tidal marsh

American elm

marsh

Turner's Creek

P S

N

0   0.25   0.5
Mile

Entrance Road

Turner's Creek Road

To (298)

© The Countryman Press

Virginia north to New Brunswick and also occurs in scattered locations on some of the Great Lakes. Beach plum has a naturally small geographic range and is restricted to sandy soils along or near the shore—the same places favored by coastal resorts and beachfront developers. About half its available habitat has been destroyed, and much of its remaining habitat is fragmented. It is considered critically imperiled in Maryland; the plums on the natural resources management area are one of twelve known populations in the state.

The best known by far of the region's rare species is the bald eagle. The river shore is the home of two adults that use the area to raise their young. Their nest is in a large, old tree at the forest edge. The site overlooks the broad slopes that lead down to the Sassafras, where the eagles teach their young to fish for food. The nest has been used since at least 1983, and most years have seen the successful fledging of young eaglets. The recovery of bald eagles here and elsewhere is one of the great successes of land managers working under the authority of the Endangered Species Act. Once listed as endangered, bald eagles are now classified as threatened by both the federal and Maryland state governments. Populations are not yet fully recovered, but the bald eagle is no longer on the brink of extinction.

The fourth rare species—Puritan tiger beetle—is an inconspicuous insect, one of the many "humbler . . . animals that form the warp and weft of [our] fraying natural fabric," as nature essayist Carolyn V. Platt describes the small, half-visible but essential components of our fauna. Like the eagles, the beetles fly around, but they are less likely to be noticed. Adult beetles are only about half an inch long, greenish copper or greenish bronze in color, and with a pattern of wide spots. Although small, they are one of the top insect predators on the beach—hence their comparison to tigers. Adults hunt by chasing after tiny flies and ants at breakneck speed and then pause, apparently to relocate their prey. This hallmark behavior of running and flying interspersed with stopping and looking has led researchers to believe that tiger beetles move so swiftly they cannot see to follow their prey. Stopping periodically does not seem to interfere with their success in hunting. They are so fast that they still bring down their quarry.

Puritan tiger beetle larvae are also predacious, but they capture their food from ambush. The larva digs a small tunnel on the face of a sandy cliff. Once safely inside, it uses its flat head to plug the opening. It attacks unsuspecting insects when they wander too close. The larva uses hooks

Windblown leaves and tide-borne water grasses meet on a beach along the Sassafras River in Sassafras Natural Resources Management Area.

along its sides as anchors to prevent it from being dragged out of its burrow.

Puritan tiger beetles are found only in places that have narrow, sandy beaches with adjacent steep cliffs of sand and clay with little vegetation. The adults live on the beach and the larvae live on the cliff face. This combination of landforms exists in only a few places in North America, so Puritan tiger beetles have never been common. However, they are far less common now than before, mostly due to habitat destruction and increased human pressures. Beetle beaches also are favored places for humans to gather for swimming and picnicking, and where eroding cliffs are being stabilized with walls and riprap to save waterfront property.

The normal life cycle of Puritan tiger beetles is two to three years, but only about one month of this time is spent as an adult. Adult beetles emerge around the middle or end of June, and by the end of July their numbers begin to decline. The larval stage, then, is the chief stage of this species. Their cliff homes are susceptible to avalanches and severe erosion.

The larvae ride out the winter in their tunnels, often by burrowing deeper. Larval mortality is high on the precarious cliffs in severe winters.

If the Puritan tiger beetle is to survive, its best chances are probably in Maryland, where it is found along the Sassafras and also across the Chesapeake Bay at Calvert Cliffs State Park. Together, the sites harbor the highest number of Puritan tiger beetles left on earth. The insect is known from only two other locations, both along the Connecticut River, one in Connecticut and one in Massachusetts. The site in Massachusetts had only about one hundred adults during the last census. The Connecticut colony is larger. Historically, the species has been recorded from five other states—New Hampshire, Vermont, New Jersey, New York, and Virginia—but is believed to be extinct in all those localities.

The U.S. Fish and Wildlife Service, which has placed the beetle on its threatened list, and the Maryland Department of Natural Resources are cooperating on a Puritan tiger beetle recovery effort. The Maryland Girl Scout Council, with the help of The Nature Conservancy, proposed a cliff stabilization project at one of the Girl Scout camps on the Sassafras where the beetle is found. The result was protection for the beetles and education for the campers: their theme for the summer session was "Beetlemania." In Maryland, there is hope for this extremely rare and remarkable native.

The trails on Sassafras Natural Resources Management Area are rough, unmarked, and sometimes poorly maintained. Be prepared to bushwhack in places. There are no visitor amenities. Hunting is allowed in season, so exercise caution when hunters are afield. Hunting is not allowed on Sunday in Maryland.

Access

From Chestertown, drive north on MD 213 for 9.7 miles to the junction with MD 298. Turn left (west). Go 1.2 miles and turn right (north) onto Turner's Creek Road. Drive for 1.7 miles and turn left (west) onto the dirt entrance road to Sassafras Natural Resources Management Area. Drive 0.7 mile and park your car in the dirt lot on the right.

Trail

A gated double track goes slightly uphill at the back of the parking area. The lane leads through agricultural fields and follows a utility line and a wide hedgerow. The hedgerow is filled with insects, birds, and other wildlife seeking the shelter and food provided by a rich array of fruiting plants such as mulberry, grape, flowering dogwood, chokecherry, and redbud.

Soon the hedgerow is left behind and the lane is surrounded by field crops. Agriculture remains the dominant land use in the area, as it has since colonial times. More than 40 percent of the 991-acre area is leased to farmers, who grow corn, soybeans, and wheat. The state buys acres of standing corn each year and leaves it in the fields as a food source for overwintering waterfowl.

Reach a major junction, with farm lanes going both left and right and an overgrown trail leading off to the right rear. The utility line leads down the lane to the right. You will return to this spot later, but for now continue straight on the double track across agricultural fields.

Another hedgerow begins on the left and a woodlot is seen on the right. Come to a fork, with a lane curving slightly to the right and another lane going more sharply to the left. A giant, vine-covered American elm stands in the fork. Take the left prong, walking under the elm's big boughs and keeping its trunk on your right. You will continue to pass agricultural fields, but you will also notice that some of the plants along the lane are probably escapees from old gardens: mimosa, rose of Sharon, red cedar, and others.

The way leads to an abandoned lodge with a few outbuildings. The dwelling is closed, but you can gain your first view of the Sassafras River from the front porch. While on the porch, look straight ahead; slightly to the left, at about the 11 o'clock position, is a rough path through the brush. Follow it, but be prepared to bushwhack a short distance through multiflora rose and other encroaching vegetation. Some of the plants bordering the path are boxwood, another species left over from when this old home place was kept as a garden. By taking the right fork on the path, you will come out onto an opening at the top of a high cliff. Be careful not to get too close to the edge. The sand cliffs are unstable and may give way without warning.

Standing on the high ground, facing northwest, you can see across the broad river and all the way downstream to the Chesapeake Bay. The elevation here is about 50 feet—hardly among the tall mountains, but in January the winds can drive you back into the shelter of the woods. The sheer cliff below you is critical larval habitat for Puritan tiger beetles.

Make your way back through the boxwood and turn right to descend a steep path to the beach. A dense, dark stand of three-story-high bamboo is on the left. The little, sandy, crescent-shaped beach on the Sassafras is a good place to rest a while and enjoy the quiet solitude. Hulbert Footner wrote, "The Sassafras is the most beautiful of Eastern Shore Rivers."

Captain John Smith and his crew were the first nonindigenous people to visit the river. They sailed from Jamestown in 1608 on a voyage to explore the Chesapeake Bay. Smith traveled upriver to at least as far as what is today Turner's Creek, where he and his men met a small band of natives and enjoyed a feast with dancing, singing, and gift-giving. Smith described their village as being "mantelled with the bark of trees." He mapped the area and named the river Tockwogh after the tribe.

From the beach, turn and retrace your steps up the steep slope, past the old lodge, by the giant elm, all the way back to the trail junction in the farm fields. Choose the rough, grassy path that leaves the intersection at about the 11 o'clock position. It begins at the head of a wooded ravine marked by a grove of black locust. There is also a post here with the number 2 on it. The way follows a weedy swath between an agricultural field on your right and a forest on your left. It winds around the bottomland that drops off precipitously to the left to Turner's Creek below. The only variation you will encounter along the way is when the grassy swath goes straight for about 0.3 mile through an old field planted recently in pines. The farm field is off to your right, and you will eventually get back to the edge between crops and trees. The pine plantation is an effort by the state to increase the riparian forest buffer above Turner's Creek. It is also designed to fill the indentations in the existing forest outline, thus reducing the amount of forest edge and increasing the proportion of deep woods. Uninterrupted trees are important for many wildlife, especially those forest interior dwelling species like migratory Neotropical songbirds.

The way leaves the agricultural field and enters a scrubby woods. Keep straight on the path and reach an old concrete parking area. Walk straight across the patchy cement to a drive that leads out to Turner's Creek Road. Turn right and walk 0.2 mile to the dirt entrance road. Turn right and walk 0.7 mile to your waiting car.

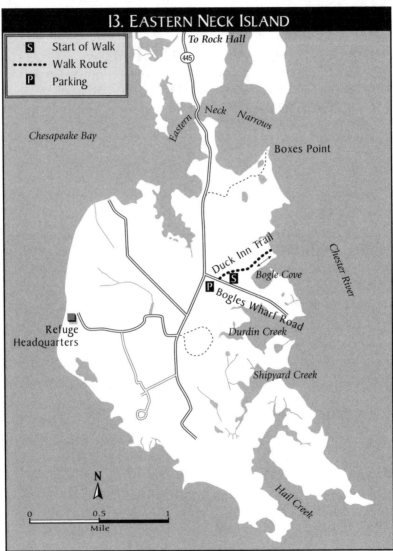

13. EASTERN NECK ISLAND

S Start of Walk
•••••• Walk Route
P Parking

To Rock Hall

445

Eastern Neck Narrows

Chesapeake Bay

Boxes Point

Duck Inn Trail

Chester River

S

Bogle Cove

P *Bogles Wharf Road*

Durdin Creek

Refuge Headquarters

Shipyard Creek

Hail Creek

N

0   0.5   1
Mile

© The Countryman Press

13. Eastern Neck Island

A walk through an island refuge to an isolated shore on the Chester River

Hiking distance: 1 mile
Hiking time: 0.75 hour
Maps: USGS Langford Creek; refuge map

Eastern Neck Island illustrates the contiguity and contrast between the natural and the overcivilized world. If you stand at the edge of the Chesapeake Bay on the island's northwestern shore on a clear day, the industrial smokestacks that ring Baltimore are visible across the water. Eastern Neck's immediate neighbor across the Chester River to the southwest, Kent Island, anchors the eastern end of the Chesapeake Bay Bridge. Because of this connection to major population centers, Kent wrestles with the stresses of traffic congestion, noise pollution, and land and waterfront development (see the next hike).

By contrast, Eastern Neck Island, with a history of human habitation stretching back at least three thousand years, remains a wild land where the patterns of nature assert themselves with striking clarity. It is a haven for resident and migrating wildlife. The island's tranquil inlets and coves, tidal flats, open fields, woodlands, and great expanses of marshlands support a remarkable diversity and abundance of life. The island is designated as a Wetlands of International Importance under the Ramsar Convention.

Eastern Neck Island's forests are one of the few remaining isolated habitats for Delmarva fox squirrel. These large squirrels, a subspecies of the eastern fox squirrel, are found only on the Delmarva Peninsula and are listed as an endangered species by the federal government. Rare birds found on the island include bald eagle, listed as threatened.

Perhaps the most spectacular wildlife scene enjoyed by most visitors, and the one for which Eastern Neck is noted, is the gathering of thousands of tundra swans that winter on the island each year. These stately swans are but a part of the large numbers of waterfowl that use the area. Canada goose, bufflehead, American wigeon, pintail, mallard, American black duck, canvasback, lesser scaup, ruddy duck, long-tailed duck, and white-winged scoter can be seen between October and March. Waterfowl populations usually peak in November.

The preservation of the 2,285-acre island was assured in 1962 when the area was set aside as the Eastern Neck National Wildlife Refuge. As part of the wildlife management program, only certain areas of the island are open to visitors. The area through which this hike passes is usually open but is closed during the public white-tailed deer and wild turkey hunts. Generally, the hunts are scheduled for eight or ten days in October, November, and April or May. Hunting is prohibited on Sunday in Maryland. Telephone the refuge office at 410-639-7056 prior to your hike during hunting season. Refuge personnel can also provide you with maps, checklists, and information on other trails. The headquarters building is located beyond the turnoff for the hike and is marked by signs. If the office is closed, limited brochures may be available at the trailhead to the Wildlife Trail, the refuge's interpretive path located on the left of the main refuge road just beyond Bogles Wharf Road.

If possible, hike this trail during the cooler months. Not only will you likely be rewarded by some memorable waterfowl sightings, but you will also avoid the numerous mosquitoes, deerflies, no-see-ums, and ticks. On Eastern Neck, these biting arthropods can turn any hike into a gauntlet. If you visit the island in the warmer seasons, wear repellent.

Access

Eastern Neck Island lies in the upper Chesapeake at the mouth of the Chester River. It is connected to the mainland by bridge. To reach the island, drive south from Chestertown on MD 20 for 12.9 miles to the shipbuilding community of Rock Hall. There, turn left (south) on MD 445 for

The wide Duck Inn Trail threads between pine forests and salt marshes on Eastern Neck Island.

the drive down Eastern Neck. After 5.7 miles you will approach the bridge across Eastern Neck Narrows. Continue straight for another 1.1 miles, then turn left onto Bogles (or Bogle's) Wharf Road. After 0.1 mile, park your car in the gravel lot on the right. A sign here points to the Duck Inn Trail.

Trail

The Duck Inn Trail begins across the road (opposite the parking lot) and meanders through the woods in a northeasterly direction. Initially the way is heavily shaded by pines, oaks, sweet gum, and flowering dogwood. This stretch of the trail is a good place to see woodpeckers and migrating warblers. Eventually, you enter a field where the path goes through tall grasses.

Marshland or open water is occasionally visible on either side of the trail. After about 0.5 mile, you enter another wooded area and then arrive at a small beach along the Chester River. The sandy beach has interspersed seams of pebbles and old oyster shells. It is a lovely, secluded shore, a place where, as Henry David Thoreau wrote, you "shall hear only the wind whispering among the reeds."

Your first impression undoubtedly will be of the river—here, a great 2-mile-wide tidal arm of the bay. The Chester is the last free-flowing river to enter the Chesapeake. It has escaped damming and channelization, and its bottomlands, bordering swamps, and nontidal wetlands have not been ditched and drained. Some boats may be on the water, and you will be able to see a few minor evidences of civilization, such as fields and dwellings, on the opposite shore, but by and large your view is of a pristine landscape little changed in thousands of years. Take time to explore the beach and surroundings. The longer you stay, the more you will discover.

The scattered, weathered shells at your feet are the remains of a midden, a trash heap of discarded oysters left by the island's prehistoric inhabitants. Indians from the Early Woodland period, stretching from about three thousand to four thousand years ago, probably used this shore as a dump while gathering oysters from the river. Disturbing or destroying this and other archaeological sites on the refuge is strictly forbidden.

From the end of the trail, a short walk to the left leads to an inlet surrounded by a broad marsh. Walking right brings you to a point that affords a sweeping view of Bogle Cove, one of the myriad indented hideaways lining the Chester. After you feel sufficiently braced by the fresh air, ancient history, and stirring beauty of these shores, turn and retrace your way.

14. Terrapin Nature Park

Off the road on Kent Island

Hiking distance: 2.75 miles
Hiking time: 1.5 hours
Map: USGS Kent Island

Kent Island is the largest island in the Chesapeake Bay. It lies just off the Eastern Shore where the bay constricts to one of its narrowest widths—the Chesapeake is only about 3 miles across between the island and Sandy Point. Its location means that Kent has always served as a gateway to the Eastern Shore for those approaching from the west. Before 1952, that meant travel by boat. In that year, the Chesapeake Bay Bridge opened to traffic and Kent became tied by steel and asphalt to the population centers on the western shore.

Unlike Eastern Neck Island, its wild neighbor to the north (see the previous chapter), Kent Island is dotted with towns, communities, subdivisions, multilane highways, commercial districts, marinas, and waterfront developments. Nevertheless, Kent Island remains a good place to hike and to enjoy scenes of the Chesapeake, its marshes and coves, and its bordering uplands. This happy result is the work of the Queen Anne's County Department of Parks and Recreation, which operates 11 landings and 12 parks totaling almost 900 acres on Kent Island. More are planned.

Included in the Kent Island dozen are the requisite golf course and skate park, but mostly the holdings are natural areas, trails, and neighborhood parks. One of the largest of the Queen Anne's County parks—275-acre Terrapin Nature Park—is the location for this hike. Set aside for passive recreation, Terrapin Nature Park protects almost 1 mile of bay

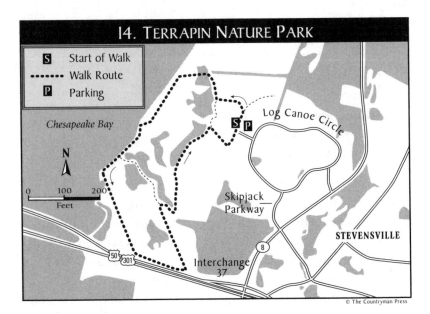

14. Terrapin Nature Park

S Start of Walk
•••••• Walk Route
P Parking

Chesapeake Bay

Log Canoe Circle

S **P**

N

0   100   200
Feet

Skipjack Parkway

STEVENSVILLE

8

50 301   Interchange 37

© The Countryman Press

shore and 73 acres of tidal wetlands. Dogs are not permitted in the park, and swimming at the beach is prohibited.

Access

Terrapin Nature Park is in Stevensville. On Kent Island, turn off US 50/ US 301 at interchange 37 and head north on MD 8. Drive for 0.3 mile to the first traffic signal and turn left onto Skipjack Parkway. Go 0.2 mile to a T-junction with Log Canoe Circle. Turn left at the stop sign and drive 0.3 mile to the entrance to Terrapin Nature Park on the left.

Trail

Begin on the paved Cross Island Trail, which leaves from the rear of the parking lot. The 6-mile Cross Island Trail is a county park that, as its name implies, traverses the east-west axis of the island. Its western terminus is here at Terrapin Nature Park. Beyond a picnic area on the right, the Cross Island Trail curves right and the Oyster Chaff Trail—covered with broken oyster shells—forks to the left. Take the Oyster Chaff Trail. Immediately on the right is an overlook of an old field that is being restored to a meadow environment of native grasses and wildflowers. Plans call for a trail system through the meadow once the new plantings have taken hold.

After the overlook, the trail splits. Keep right, and soon you will reach the North Blind, a wildlife observation station that looks out onto a tidal marsh.

The marsh is home for the park's namesake, the diamondback terrapin, the only species of turtle in North America that lives in brackish water. Named for the diamond-shaped scutes (plates) of their carapace (top shell), diamondback terrapins are well adapted for life in salt water because of their low skin permeability and strongly webbed feet. But they like to bask on mud flats or logs during warm weather, and they can sometimes be seen in the marsh. The females also come to land to nest from May to July. They dig shallow holes in beach sand above the high-tide line and lay 4–18 eggs. Diamondback terrapins live for 25–40 years, and populations are still recovering from overharvesting during the early 20th century. Diamondbacks have been eaten since at least colonial days, but from the 1880s through the 1920s turtle meat was considered a gourmet delicacy—the main ingredient in terrapin soup, laced with cream and sherry. Wild populations in many areas were decimated to supply expensive restaurants. In 1891, some 89,000 pounds of terrapin were taken from Maryland waters. (An average female weighs about 1 pound; males are smaller). Terrapins were not only eaten in this country. They were exported to France, Germany, and Brazil, where wealthy rubber barons in the Amazon city of Manaus feasted on them during the boom times before World War I.

The diamondback trade collapsed during the Great Depression. Diamondback terrapin is the Maryland state reptile, but its status in the Chesapeake Bay is unknown. Current threats to its numbers come from destruction of nesting beaches, excessive predation of young turtles by

Even a fiery sunset can't warm an ice-speckled Chesapeake Bay off Kent Island.

raccoons, road kill of females, and death by drowning in submerged eel and crab pots. Maryland watermen hauled in 676 pounds of terrapins in 2004.

After searching the marsh for diamondbacks and other wildlife, walk on toward North Beach and an exhibit at a gazebo. A short, sandy path leaves the Oyster Chaff Trail and leads through low dunes and scattered beach grass to reach the water. The vista before you is dominated by the Chesapeake Bay Bridge and the string of vehicles crossing it, but it also includes the driftwood-studded beach, expansive views up, down, and across the bay, and likely some gulls patrolling the high-tide line.

Back on the main route, you soon cross an inlet connecting the tidal marsh with the bay. Beyond the crossing, South Beach on trail-right is bulwarked against shore erosion.

The path forks, with the left fork leading back to the parking lot. Take the wide right prong—the South Meadow Loop—and continue walking along the bay shore.

A grassy promontory on the right has a bench where you can sit and rest. This small rise, with scattered black locust, black cherry, and red cedar, affords the best view yet of the bridge. The first span was opened in 1952, immediately putting the ferry between Matapeake and Sandy Point out of business. The name was changed to the William Preston Lane Jr. Memorial Bridge in 1967 to honor the Maryland governor who spearheaded the construction of the crossing in the late 1940s. Just about everybody still calls it the Bay Bridge. By the mid-1960s traffic was so heavy that planning began for a second span. What are now the westbound lanes opened in 1973. More than 12 million vehicles cross the bridge every year.

The trail continues south along a field edge and veers slightly inland away from the shore. The path turns sharply left when it reaches US 50/US 301 and parallels the highway for a few hundred feet. The experience of walking close to a three-lane with traffic approaching at 65 mph (assuming that cars are not slowed to a crawl because of congestion on the bridge) is one not often found on hiking trails.

The path leaves the broken oyster shells behind and turns left, away from the highway, on an asphalted lane. The pavement soon turns right to reach a wastewater treatment plant, and you continue straight on a wide, shell-covered trail.

The wide trail continues straight through fields, but you turn right onto a narrow path, also with oyster shells, into the woods. This is the first trail to the right since leaving the asphalt. Big oaks and American holly dominate the forest. The way soon descends slightly to cross a tidal wetlands on wooden bridges.

The route winds through the forest and passes a maintenance area on the right. The way goes through a very young, scrubby forest, with the tree trunks resembling giant matchsticks—straight and thin. Come to a T-junction; the way to the left leads to the South Blind, but here turn right to get back to the trailhead.

As you skirt a big field, you can see the two-story brick buildings of the Chesapeake Business Park. Your shell-covered trail curves right just after a grassy trail comes in from the left. Pass an old barn on the right and come again to the parking lot.

15. Tuckahoe State Park

A loop featuring ridgetop and bottomland forests

Hiking distance: 8.25 miles
Hiking time: 4 hours
Maps: USGS Ridgely; park map

Tuckahoe State Park surrounds the upper watershed of Tuckahoe Creek, a tranquil tributary of the Choptank River. The park protects the forks of the Tuckahoe (where German Branch and Mason Branch join) and approximately the first 7 miles of the creek. The Tuckahoe is dammed in the park to create a small lake, but most of the stream runs free and quiet through a jungled floodplain of tall trees and swamp thickets.

Tuckahoe is a variation of *Tockwogh*, the name given by John Smith to an upper Chesapeake Bay river that is today the Sassafras. Smith wrote that the natives in the region called themselves the Tockwogh. The Indians may have been referring to a large aquatic plant with arrowhead-shaped leaves that is often found near slow-moving creeks, rivers, and ponds throughout Eastern North America. This robust perennial, whose common name is still tuckahoe, was an important food and medicine to many Native American peoples. The seeds were reportedly eaten like peas, and the rootstalk, large and rich in starch, was dried and ground into flour for making bread and soups. The roots were also used to treat maladies. Gladys Tantaquidgeon, an early ethnobotanist, recorded how the Nanticoke used grated tuckahoe root in milk to give to sick babies.

Gathering tuckahoe rootstalk must have been laborious. The plant grows in muck, and the root can extend down 1.5 feet and weigh up to 6 pounds. Once the rootstalk is extracted, processing it requires lots of time and careful preparation. Tuckahoe, like other members of the arum family such as jack-in-the-pulpit and skunk cabbage, is rich in calcium oxalate, a toxic compound. Eating such plants unprocessed has been described as "having your mouth and digestive tract stuck with hundreds of tiny needles." Thorough cooking and drying are needed to destroy the calcium oxalate.

Tuckahoe seeds, seasonal and relatively small, did not provide the same nutritional bulk as the roots, but they were easier to harvest. The dark green to black seeds could be picked from the tall stalks in late summer. Once ripe and fallen, the seeds are buoyant and are commonly found along shorelines many miles from their place of origin—even out to sea.

Tuckahoe is no longer as popular with human consumers as it once was, but it remains an important component of healthy aquatic ecosystems. It and other big herbaceous plants are used to measure the well-being of swamps and other wetlands. Aquatic ecologists estimate that tuckahoe accounts for up to 5 tons per acre of total plant production in tidal freshwater wetlands, and that does not include the belowground biomass of the immense and dense roots. Beds of tuckahoe are very important as spawning areas for anadromous fishes. The fleshy seeds are food for many birds, including rails, wood duck, and American black duck (hence another common name for the plant—duck corn). Beaver feed on the roots, leaves, and stems.

At 3,800 acres, Tuckahoe is the largest of the state parks on the Maryland Eastern Shore. Along with the adjacent Adkins Arboretum, it is also one of the best places to hike, with a trail network that exceeds 15 miles. The walk described here passes through some of the most scenic areas along Tuckahoe Creek. There is great variety along the way: wooded ridges, a meandering stream, lush bottomlands, darting and scurrying wildlife, spring wildflowers, fall foliage colors, winter snow and ice patterns. The trail is well marked and maintained and is shared by hikers, mountain bikers, and horseback riders. A detailed trail map is for sale in the visitor center.

The coast-to-coast American Discovery Trail passes through Tuckahoe State Park, and there is a backcountry shelter for use by long-distance hikers. Hunting is allowed in some parts of the park; use care if you are hiking here during hunting season. Note that Maryland law prohibits

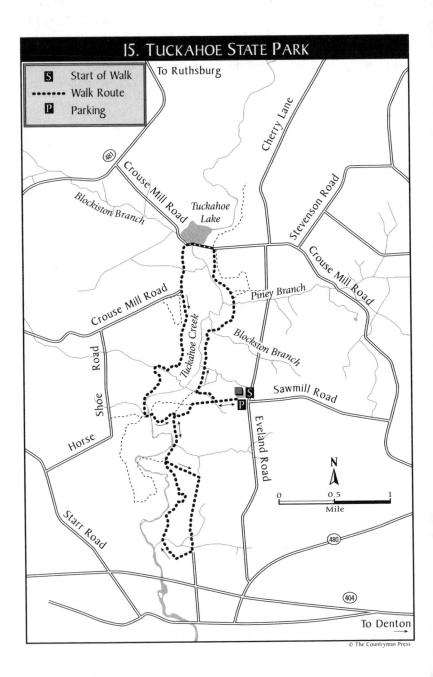

15. TUCKAHOE STATE PARK

S Start of Walk
•••••• Walk Route
P Parking

To Ruthsburg

Cherry Lane

Stevenson Road

481

Crouse Mill Road

Blockiston Branch

Tuckahoe Lake

Crouse Mill Road

Piney Branch

Crouse Mill Road

Blockston Branch

Crouse Mill Road

Tuckahoe Creek

Horse Shoe Road

Sawmill Road

S
P

Eveland Road

N

0   0.5   1
Mile

Starr Road

480

404

To Denton

© The Countryman Press

hunting on Sunday. Some low trails along Tuckahoe Creek may be flooded during periods of high water. Call the park at 410-820-1668 to check on conditions.

Access

From Denton, drive west on MD 404 for 6.0 miles. Turn right (east) onto MD 480, go just 0.1 mile, and turn left onto Eveland Road. Drive for 1.7 miles to the Tuckahoe State Park visitor center and office on the left.

If coming from Centreville, drive east on MD 304 for 6.5 miles to Ruthsburg. Turn right (south) on MD 481. After 2.0 miles, enter Tuckahoe State Park by turning left onto Crouse Mill Road. The road crosses Blockiston Branch upstream of Tuckahoe Lake and then curves left where a side road (also called Crouse Mill Road) goes right. Follow the leftmost Crouse Mill Road and cross Tuckahoe Creek downstream of Tuckahoe Lake. Turn right onto Eveland Road (1.6 miles from MD 481). Go 1.4 miles to the visitor center and office on the right.

Trail

Head out on the Tuckahoe Office Spur Trail, which follows a gravel lane at the back of the small parking lot. Keep the visitor center (an old farmhouse) on your right and walk between outbuildings. The trail, marked by a white blaze with a blue dot, goes straight across farm fields.

When you reach the woods, the Tuckahoe Office Spur Trail forks left and the Arboretum Spur Trail (marked by a white blaze with a red dot) goes right. You will return to this junction later, but for now keep right on the Arboretum Spur Trail.

Your path descends along a miry swale lined with American sycamore. The waters in the swale work their way west and eventually form a distinguishable channel. The little run carves a modest ravine and begins to cut a deeper course to join Tuckahoe Creek. In the driest of weather this stream still holds enough water to sustain a wetland and riparian plant community. During spring floods it gushes about in all directions, rearranging the alluvial soils and giving the bottomland a face-lift. Before your trail leads away from the stream, you will see that the water has down-cut a sizable hollow. On your next visit, you may find the ravine even deeper and extending farther upstream.

The Arboretum Spur Trail angles right, away from the ravine, and intersects the Tuckahoe Valley Trail at a T-junction. Turn right.

The 4.5-mile, blue-blazed Tuckahoe Valley Trail is the longest trail in the park. It is the major footpath along the creek's left bank. Here you are walking upstream and soon enter Adkins Arboretum. Initially established as the State Arboretum by the Maryland Department of Natural Resources in 1980, Adkins Arboretum is now a not-for-profit organization promoting the conservation of the native flora of the Delmarva Peninsula. Walking along the Tuckahoe Valley Trail will give you a small glimpse of the 400-acre arboretum's extensive exhibits and displays. Much more is available, including opportunities to view wetlands, stream bottoms, deciduous forests, coniferous forests, and old fields being restored to indigenous grasses and wildflowers. The visitor center, off your path and accessible by car from Eveland Road, has information on tours, events, and educational programs.

Pass the first intersection with the Tuckahoe Creekside Walk on the left and come to a narrow lane (the Blockston Branch Walk) where your trail curves to the left. Numbered posts along the way are keyed to a self-guiding tour brochure on bottomland forest ecology available at the arboretum visitor center. Your trail follows part of the tour in descending order (13, 12, 11, etc.). The other end of the Tuckahoe Creekside Walk intersects from the left.

Continue straight on the broad Tuckahoe Valley Trail where the Blockston Branch Walk goes right. (You could reach the visitor center on foot by following the Blockston Branch Walk). Cross Blockston Branch on a wide bridge. The stream, although small, has a sizable floodplain. On the other side, the trail climbs a short rise. A side trail (the Ridge Walk) goes right, and the broad lane continues straight as the Upland Walk, but you stay on the Tuckahoe Valley Trail by turning left onto a narrow single track.

The path descends to near Piney Branch and a junction with a con-

The soft sound of gently flowing water accompanies hikers as they cross Tuckahoe Creek in Tuckahoe State Park.

necting trail that leads right uphill to the North Meadow. The trail soon crosses the stream on a wooden bridge and leaves Adkins Arboretum. At the time of my last visit, Piney Branch was home to an active beaver colony. A dam, a bank lodge, and lots of gnawed and stripped branches are evidence that the big, nocturnal rodents live in the stream.

The Tuckahoe Valley Trail passes the two entrances to the Piney Branch Loop Trail on the right and, after about another 0.5 mile, reaches the back of the Tuckahoe Trail Shelter at the edge of a big field. The three-sided shelter faces the American Discovery Trail (ADT) and is used by hikers traveling the transcontinental route. The ADT follows the Equestrian Cutoff Trail through most of the park but joins with your trail as you reach Crouse Mill Road.

The Tuckahoe Valley Trail ends at Crouse Mill Road. Turn left on the paved road, which is also the route of the American Discovery Trail. A pine-shaded picnic area is on the right, on the shore of Tuckahoe Lake. Cross Tuckahoe Creek just below the dam and spillway.

After about 0.25 mile, turn south (left) on the first paved road (also called Crouse Mill Road) past the creek. The American Discovery Trail continues west (straight) on Crouse Mill Road on its way to California.

Walk along the shoulder for about 0.5 mile, past the entrance to the Tuckahoe Equestrian Center on the right at the top of a low hill. Where the road curves right, continue straight on the narrow, orange-blazed Pee Wee's Trail. The way climbs steeply at first but then levels as it runs along a terrace above the Tuckahoe Creek floodplain. You are now proceeding downstream on the right bank. The trees are young and scrubby where a connecting bridle trail comes in from the right, but soon you enter a mature forest filled with a rich diversity of big trees such as black oak, white oak, sour gum, sweet gum, mockernut hickory, beech, sassafras, and tulip tree. The shrub layer is also profuse, with American holly, greenbriers, flowering dogwood, poison ivy, honeysuckles, ironwood, and burning bush.

Tuckahoe Creek is visible on the left, although at times of high water the main channel is obscured and the entire bottomland serves as a floodway. Beaver are plentiful in this area; you can see their mud-stained paths leading between the water and gnawed trees along the trail.

The route rises, falls, and weaves in and out of the woods, sometimes leading along the edges of fields and forests and crossing small tributaries. The way is well marked with painted orange blazes on trees and posts. Pee Wee's Trail fords a small stream and ends at a T-junction with Greiner's Fishing Trail near a bridge across the creek. This area may be flooded during periods of high water.

Turn left on Greiner's Fishing Trail and cross Tuckahoe Creek on an arched bridge. On the other side, come immediately to a T-intersection with the blue-blazed Tuckahoe Valley Trail. Turn right, continuing downstream, but now on the left bank.

As you begin a slight ascent out of the soggy bottom, a side path (a high-water route for the Tuckahoe Valley Trail) comes in from the left. Your way continues straight uphill by following an old, brick-strewn roadway to Wilbur's Cutoff Trail on the left. You will return to this junction later, but for now stay on the Tuckahoe Valley Trail by curving to the right.

The way passes through a part of the park that has been farmed fairly recently. Small trees, planted pines, old household dumps, and invasive plants characterize the landscape. After crossing a stream on a wooden bridge, reach a major trail junction. The Turkey Hill Trail goes right and the Creekside Cliff Trail continues straight. You will return to this spot later along the Creekside Cliff Trail, but for now stay on the blue-blazed Tuckahoe Valley Trail by turning left.

The path leads through a pine plantation and then enters a scrubland of almost impenetrable honeysuckles and grapes. The trail tunnels through the thicket and crosses a small stream on a wooden bridge.

Come to a power line and cross a stream on a wooden bridge in the right-of-way. Multiflora rose forms dense thickets of thorny tangles all around the bridge. Immediately on the other side of the bridge, turn right onto the yellow-blazed Creekside Cliff Trail. The Tuckahoe Valley Trail continues ahead to the southern boundary of the park.

The Creekside Cliff Trail follows the electric line for a short distance and then turns right to leave the right-of-way. The path passes through another honeysuckle thicket before crossing a small stream on a wooden bridge. The Creekside Cliff Trail, as its name implies, follows a high, wooded bluff above the Tuckahoe Creek bottom. The steep drop-off to the left of the trail is unusually spectacular for the flat Eastern Shore.

The Creekside Cliff Trail comes to the junction with the Turkey Hill Trail and the Tuckahoe Valley Trail encountered earlier in the hike. Continue straight on the Tuckahoe Valley Trail and retrace your route to the top of the old, brick-strewn road. There turn right onto Wilbur's Cutoff Trail.

The path leads straight along rows of pines and reaches a T-intersection with the Tuckahoe Office Spur Trail. Turn right. Arrive back at the junction with the Arboretum Spur Trail that you reached very early in the hike and continue straight across farm fields to the visitor center parking lot.

16. Martinak State Park

A loop through land rich in Indian lore, featuring two spurs to overlooks of the Choptank River and Watts Creek

Hiking distance: 2 miles
Hiking time: 1 hour
Map: USGS Hobbs

Few of the world's coastlines are as convoluted and complex as the Chesapeake shore. The land was drowned by rising ocean waters at the end of the last ice age, and today's result, especially on the Eastern Shore, is a fantastic assemblage of creeks, rivers, coves, small bays, sounds, straits, and islands. The Delmarva Peninsula is about 200 miles long, and yet within this short span there are no fewer than 21 rivers flowing into the bay. They are generally short, arising sluggishly in upland swamps and soon broadening into expansive tidal estuaries. The greatest of these rivers is the Choptank.

Martinak State Park lies along the upper reaches of the Choptank River. It is very popular with fishermen, who go after the catfish and bluegill, and with boaters, who use it as a jumping-off point. Campers and picnickers also enjoy the park. Martinak is also a pleasant setting for a short walk on the park's nature and physical fitness trails or on a few unmarked paths.

The hike featured here follows informal paths connecting the developed portions of the park—the picnic areas, boat ramp, nature center, amphitheater, and campground—and portions of the physical fitness trail and Lost Pond Nature Trail. It is impossible to get lost for long in this small, 108-acre park, but some of the trails become confusing when passing through these areas. Read the directions carefully. Mosquitoes are abundant in the woods in the summer. Dogs are not permitted in any part of Martinak.

Along the way, look for partridgeberry, moccasin flower, Venus's looking glass, and other wildflowers. In the forest, wild grapes climb toward the sunlight, while big, tall pines dominate the canopy. The deep woods provide protection for many reptiles, birds, and small mammals, including eastern hognose snake, whip-poor-will, at least three species of owls, and eastern gray squirrel. It is one of the best places I know to see fish crows. American crows are also common, so Martinak is a good park to practice your skill in separating the two similar species.

The area that is now parkland may have been the site of a native village in olden days. Projectile points, shards, and other artifacts are commonly found in the vicinity. In historic times, a Choptank Indian reservation was downriver, where Secretary Creek enters. A major Indian trail also was known to have passed nearby or maybe through this area, carrying hunters, traders, and warriors between the upper Choptank and the Delaware River near the present-day Chesapeake & Delaware Canal (see chapter 11).

Clearly the Choptank River has been a focal point in the landscape of the Eastern Shore for human inhabitants since ancient times. Tiny bands of natives were at home on the river's banks, where they established a culture based upon farming, gathering, hunting, and fishing. They felled trees to create clearings where they grew crops of corn, squash, pumpkins, beans, and tobacco. The tree trunks were laboriously hollowed out to make canoes from which to net and spear fish and capture crustaceans and mollusks. Men of the tribe hunted in the vast wilderness for large and small game. Women and children gathered bird eggs, acorns, nuts, berries, fruits, and many different kinds of wild plants, not only for food but also for clothing, medicine, teas, and dyes. As farmers, hunters, fishermen, gatherers, even physicians, Indians fitted themselves precisely into the patterns of the land. They knew the rivers, marshes, and forests as no other people since.

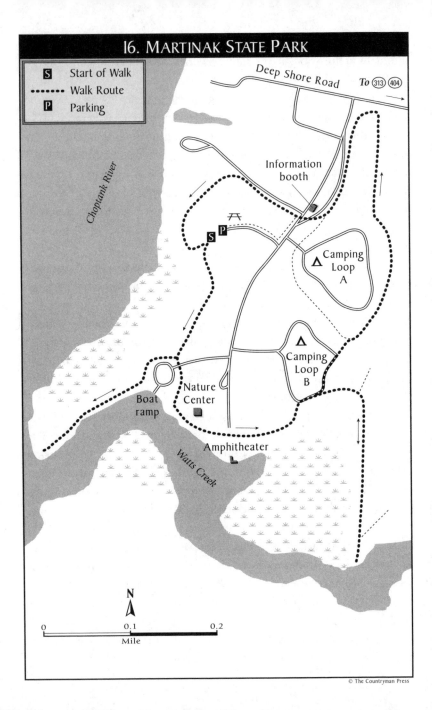

16. MARTINAK STATE PARK

S Start of Walk

····· Walk Route

P Parking

Deep Shore Road   To ③③③ ④⓪④

Choptank River

Information booth

S **P**

Camping Loop A

Camping Loop B

Nature Center

Boat ramp

Amphitheater

Watts Creek

N

0   0.1   0.2

Mile

© The Countryman Press

The peaceful tribe along the river was probably seminomadic, roving over rather large areas to hunt, fish, and trade. Other, more powerful tribes to the north (the Susquehannock and the Seneca) sometimes drove them out during raids and invasions. Yet the river remained central to their tribal culture; they molded their mind, will, and spirit to the river, and they always returned to it. The river likely represented a sparkling symbol of nature's power and permanence, serving not only as a source of food and an avenue of transportation but also, perhaps just as important, as a means of inspiration, renewal, honest counsel, and solace.

Europeans met the small tribe in the early 1600s. They learned that the natives called the wide river *Choptank,* which probably means "it flows in the opposite direction"—an apt description of the long tides that surge back and forth in the channel. The people had no name for themselves; the river and its surroundings were by and large their whole context. The English called them Choptanks. Much later, ethnologists and anthropologists would classify them as a subdivision of the Nanticoke and as belonging to the Algonquian linguistic family.

Relations between the Choptank and the English were mostly cordial. The natives adopted the metal tools, weapons, and other items offered by the whites in exchange for land. The English established a comfortable economy based largely upon growing tobacco. As the colony prospered, more settlers were attracted to the region. More land was needed, said the whites, to grow tobacco and other crops. Conflicts between the races inevitably developed. The English conceived of the land in terms of ownership and use, a way of thinking alien to the Indian.

The Choptank were soon outnumbered and outmaneuvered. Some unscrupulous whites stole land from them by guile or trickery; sometimes deals were struck after Indians were drugged with rum and whiskey. In the late 1600s, the tribe petitioned the Maryland Assembly for the land granted to them earlier by Lord Baltimore. The Choptank Reservation was created in 1698 near the present-day park. Backed into an area of only 3 square miles along a river they once ruled, the Choptank still found no peace. An Indian delegation complained to the governor in 1759 that

Watts Creek flows into the broad Choptank River in Martinak State Park.

they were suffering from a shortage of food and were being violently removed from their land.

Without a strong leader and disorganized as a people, the Choptank wandered, bewildered, mired and helpless in fear, displaced from the center of their natural world. Some became assimilated into the white or black communities developing in their old empire. When other, upriver Nanticoke took up arms against the colonists over land disputes, a general war was declared on all Indians. The peace-loving Choptank, who had no history of warfare, were caught in the middle as whites sought vengeance and retribution. A few Indians moved deeper into the marshes, huddling in isolated and remote places where they could hide from the whites; living apart from the tribe, they gradually took on the outward signs of white society. Most started a long migration to the north, joining the Iroquois in New York and Canada and becoming incorporated into that confederacy. Census figures dramatically chart the disappearance of the Choptank as a people. In 1600, an estimated 1,600 Nanticoke (including Choptank) lived on the Eastern Shore. By 1722, only about 500 remained. Seventy years later their number had dwindled to 30.

The immense river still glides on, bearing its original Indian name, thoughtless that a way of life has vanished from the earth. On the river the silence is acute. To a visitor knowing the past, the Choptank is a vital, intimate link between himself and the ancient ones who dwelled here.

Access

Martinak State Park is near Denton and can be reached by driving southeast on MD 313 and 404 for 1.9 miles. Turn right onto Deep Shore Road and then left into the park after 0.6 mile. Proceed past the information booth. At 0.2 mile from the entrance, you reach picnic area A on the right. Follow the short drive to the parking lot and leave your car. (If picnic area A is closed for the off-season, continue along the main park road a short distance to picnic area B on the right.)

Trail

Walk into picnic area A and turn left. Pass the playground (on your right) and the restrooms (on your left). Descend slightly into a ravine, cross a small stream on earthen fill, and climb up to picnic area B.

Go through picnic area B, keeping the pavilion on your left. The broad Choptank is visible on your right. At the far end of picnic area B, find a wide trail that leads through the woods, paralleling the river. The way comes out upon a paved road that is part of the park's boat launching area. A spur trail leads right at the boat ramp to this hike's first scenic overlook. Follow the maintenance road along the quay to a small, low, wooded headland. The promontory has splendid views of the Choptank River where Watts Creek flows into it. Oaks, American holly, and red cedar stand watch over the spacious river, still navigable here by large boats although you are miles from the Chesapeake.

Walk back along the quay, turn right, cross the paved boat ramp road, and climb a low bluff. A few picnic tables and benches are scattered among the trees and mowed grass on the bluff. The park's nature center and historic exhibits are also in this area. The nature center is open week-ends from the Saturday before Memorial Day to Labor Day. Keep the restrooms on your left as you walk through the grounds. On the far side of the grassy area, reach a narrow trail that enters a brushy woods above Watts Creek. Sunny areas along the bank are crowded with common mullein, its fuzzy, light green leaves ascending a tall, clublike stalk topped by yellow flowers throughout the summer. Your path leads upstream and very shortly emerges at the back of an amphitheater built over the creek.

Continue straight and enter a woods road on the far side of the amphitheater clearing. Tall loblolly pine, beech, and oaks shade the trail in this vicinity. The way curves left and comes out at the rear of campsite 9 in camping loop B. Proceed through the campsite and turn right on the paved campground road.

Walk a short distance along the pavement and turn right off the road between campsites 11 and 12 to reach a spur trail to the second scenic overlook. Find your trail at the back of campsite 12, from where it descends steeply into a ravine. Cross the little branch at the bottom on a wooden bridge. After climbing out of the ravine, reach a T-junction and turn right on a forested path that follows the boundary between the park (on the right) and Camp Mardela, a Church of the Brethren facility (on the left). The path descends another deep ravine and crosses a run at the bottom on a wooden bridge. Farther along, buildings of Camp Mardela are visible on the left. As you near Watts Creek, a wide trail comes in from the left rear. Continue straight to a quiet overlook onto a broad, winding tidal creek lined with arrowhead plants and rimmed by trees.

Retrace your steps along the quarter-mile spur trail, being careful to continue straight on the narrow way where the wide trail leads right to the church camp. Cross the ravine and turn left at the top of the rise. Descend steeply again, cross the little branch, and arrive back at campsites 11 and 12 in camping loop B. Turn right on the paved campground road.

Walk along the pavement to campsite 18 and turn right off the road between campsites 18 and 19. You will find an informal trail behind the campsites and also see some narrow ditches and a wooden bridge across one of the drainageways. The shallow ditches were dug to drain water from the forest and thereby decrease the mosquito population. These small ditches may be completely dry during periods of low rainfall. Aim for the wooden bridge, which is on the physical fitness trail, a circular trail around camping loop A. Turn right on the trail and proceed down through the numbered exercise stations (11, 10, 9, etc.). The first exercise station you will encounter is 11 (sit and stretch).

Reach station 1 at Deep Shore Road. Turn left to continue on the fitness loop as it curves left to reach the park entrance road. The trail then more or less parallels the park road on its way to the entrance of camping loop A. When you reach station 19 near the information booth, turn right and cross the entrance road. Continue straight on the Lost Pond Nature Trail.

The path soon curves left and descends steeply to cross a little stream. Climb out of the ravine and enter picnic area A, where you parked your car.

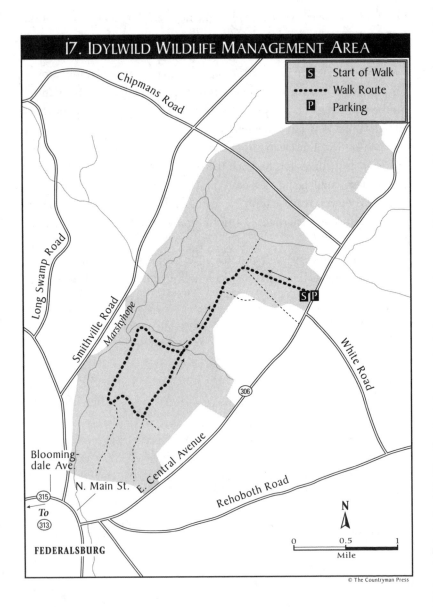

17. IDYLWILD WILDLIFE MANAGEMENT AREA

S Start of Walk

•••••• Walk Route

P Parking

Chipmans Road

Long Swamp Road

Smithville Road

Marshyhope

White Road

S P

306

Blooming-dale Ave.

E. Central Avenue

N. Main St.

Rehoboth Road

315

To

313

FEDERALSBURG

N

0   0.5   1
Mile

© The Countryman Press

17. Idylwild Wildlife Management Area

A scenic walk through upland fields and forests

Hiking distance: 6.25 miles
Hiking time: 3 hours
Maps: USGS Federalsburg and Seaford West

About 25 miles of excellent walking trails meander through the 3,300-acre Idylwild Wildlife Management Area. Hikers, equestrians, bird watchers, wildflower enthusiasts, and sportsmen use the area, and canoeists and kayakers paddle down Marshyhope Creek on the western boundary in spring at high water. Visitor usage, however, is slight; Idylwild is a good place to walk if you are seeking quietness and solitude. The lack of amenities such as picnic tables and restrooms means the area is less disturbed by crowds of people.

Idylwild sits astride an ancient dune system, a narrow belt of sandy terrain left over from the time when the Chesapeake shoreline was nearby. Old sand dunes are found scattered over much of the Delmarva Peninsula, but they are particularly well developed here along the east side of Marshyhope Creek. When sea levels dropped during the last ice age, the shore dunes were left behind and stranded far inland. The timeworn dunes are gently sloping sandy ridges created 13,000 to 30,000 years ago out of the underlying Parsonsburg Sand Formation. The Parsonsburg Sand can be as much as 15 feet thick. The dunes are rather subtle features on the landscape, but the trails on Idylwild will remind you of the difficulties of hiking through deep sand.

The sandy soil is nutrient-poor, with low water-retention capacity. The result is a unique plant community adapted for life in dry environments. The relic dunes are usually dominated by pitch pine and oaks.

Lichens—especially reindeer moss—and true mosses are other important components of the community. Prickly pear also grows among the thickets.

The hike described here covers just a portion of the trails available. It enters the area on a long spur, loops counterclockwise around the interior, and then returns the same way. Because the hike lies entirely within a public hunting area, I recommend you plan your visit for a time other than hunting season. Hunting occurs from dawn to dusk, from Monday through Saturday, from mid-September through January and from mid-April to mid-May. Hunting is not allowed on Sunday in Maryland.

Access

From Denton, drive south on MD 313 for 14.6 miles to the vicinity of Federalsburg. Turn left onto MD 315 (Bloomingdale Avenue). Enter Federalsburg after 0.1 mile and continue on Bloomingdale Avenue, which turns to the right after 0.6 mile and becomes North Main Street. Stay on North Main Street for another 0.4 mile to the traffic signal in the center of town, and there turn left (east) on East Central Avenue. You will leave Federalsburg after 0.3 mile, and there the road becomes MD 306. Continue east, passing White Road on the right after 2.6 miles and, 0.2 mile farther, turning left into the Idylwild Wildlife Management Area parking lot.

Trail

Follow the double track that begins at the rear of the parking lot. The trail cuts across an open field before entering the forest. This field is one of several at Idylwild that are custom-farmed under lease to provide more diverse habitat for game. Crops are cultivated specifically to provide food and shelter for wild turkey, eastern cottontail, white-tailed deer, and other wildlife. Later you will occasionally encounter small clearings in the forest that are planted as game food plots. After about 0.75 mile you intersect a very broad trail at a T-junction in the woods. Turn left. Small prickly pear grows among the reindeer moss, greenbriers, and fallen needles and leaves in the vicinity of this intersection.

The wide trails in Idylwild Wildlife Management Area offer peaceful moments beneath tall pines and oaks.

The wide, sandy trail passes through a mixed forest of pines, oaks, beech, American holly, red cedar, and other trees. About 1 mile from the T-junction, the way descends very slightly to cross a small stream that flows through a large culvert under the lane. A nest box for wood duck is in the upstream swampy area on the left of the trail. The branch runs into Marshyhope Creek and eventually the Nanticoke River.

At the top of the small rise beyond the stream, a wide trail enters from the right. You will return to this place later along the trail that continues straight; for now, turn right. Your way becomes narrower and shaded almost exclusively by tall hardwoods as you skirt the bottomland on your right. After about 0.5 mile you will reach a small clearing where the trail curves left at a 90-degree angle, leaving the stream bottom behind.

The way passes through dense woodland, canopied by tall oaks and pines. American holly and mountain laurel predominate in the shrub layer. The trail meanders toward the southwest, with occasional side trails to the left and right. Stay generally straight on the main trail. After passing a clearing on the left, the trail curves gradually to the left and southeasterly. Some exceptional American holly is found in this quarter of the wildlife management area.

About 3.5 miles from the parking lot, you come out of the woods at a major trail intersection in a small clearing. A route continues more or less straight where a broad cross trail goes both left and right. A large agricultural field is to your left front and an old field is to your right front. Turn left, keeping the large field, separated from the trail by a hedgerow, on your right. You leave the farm field and hedgerow behind after about 0.25 mile when the main trail veers to the left.

Continue more or less straight on the very broad trail, ignoring narrower trails that go left and right. Walk about 0.5 mile after leaving the big field and come again to the entrance spur above the little branch. Return along the spur to reach the parking lot.

Delaware

18. Redden State Forest

Level walking in Coastal Plain forestlands

Hiking distance: 4.75 miles
Hiking time: 2.5 hours
Map: USGS Georgetown

Biologists generally recognize at least seven different forest ecosystems in North America. Of these, the Southeastern Coastal Plain forest covers a comparatively small geographic area but contains a rich array of tree species. This forest type is restricted to the Atlantic seaboard from New Jersey south to Florida and continues westward along the Gulf Coast to Texas, with a narrow band reaching northward along the Mississippi Valley to southern Illinois. Pines cover extensive parts of the forest, but oaks and hickories tend to dominate sites free of fires. Hardwoods also are found in the wet lowlands.

Delaware's Redden State Forest contains good examples of trees making up the Southeastern Coastal Plain forest. Lying along the western edge of the upland that splits the Delmarva Peninsula, the forest covers sandy and remarkably flat land. Elevations average about 48 feet above sea level and vary by only 4 feet over the entire length of this hike.

The land was extensively farmed as recently as about 70 years ago, but today the forest has reclaimed the old fields and few evidences of man's agricultural practices can be found. Redden is the largest of Delaware's three state forests. Managed primarily for timber production, the 5,500-acre forest also serves hikers, naturalists, hunters, and other outdoor enthusiasts.

Your hike is mostly on broad forest roads, but a short segment follows part of the Educational Trail, the forest's interpretive trail. Booklets keyed to numbered and lettered posts along the Educational Trail are available in the headquarters office or from a box at an information board. The numbers identify specific trees and the letters describe forest management principles or ecological concepts. Parts of the route are often wet, so hiking boots are recommended. The way passes through areas used by hunters during game seasons. The shotgun deer hunt is usually three separate weeks in November, December, and January. Use caution during these times. Delaware does not allow hunting on Sunday. Call the forest office at 302-856-2893 if you have questions.

Access

To reach the trailhead from Georgetown, drive west for 1 mile on DE 18, then turn right (north) and continue for 3 miles on US 113. Turn right onto East Redden Road (Road 565), pass through the hamlet of Redden at the railroad crossing, and then turn right onto Redden Forest Drive, the entrance road to the state forest (0.5 mile from US 113). Drive past an athletic field, a picnic area, a fishing pond, and some maintenance buildings to reach the office (the last building on the right). Park your vehicle on the right side of the office.

Trail

Keep the headquarters on your right as you walk along the entrance road to an intersection with a forest road (going left and right) and the Educational Trail (going straight). Turn left, following the sign to the lodge. You will return to this spot along the Educational Trail later in the hike. Pass around a vehicle gate and continue along the wide, gravel forest road.

Around the bend you will pass in front of a large, rambling, wooden building. Built by the Pennsylvania Railroad in 1903 as a hunting lodge, the structure is still used today by organizations who rent it from the state. The rail line that brought train cars of quail hunters to Redden runs along the western boundary of the forest, but today only Norfolk Southern freight trains travel the tracks. The Educational Trail enters from the right at the lodge and runs along with your trail for a short distance.

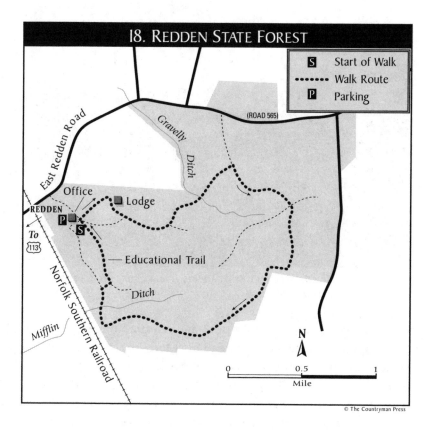

18. REDDEN STATE FOREST

S	Start of Walk
......	Walk Route
P	Parking

East Redden Road

Gravelly Ditch

(ROAD 565)

Office

REDDEN

To 113

Lodge

P

S

Educational Trail

Ditch

Mifflin

Norfolk Southern Railroad

N

0   0.5   1
Mile

© The Countryman Press

When around the lodge, continue along the shady forest road. The Educational Trail soon turns right on a single track, but stay straight on the wide lane. Pass two primitive campsites, one on the left and another, farther along, on the right. Walk around another vehicle gate and cross Gravelly Ditch as it flows under the forest road through a metal culvert.

Your walk thus far has been mainly through a mixed hardwood-evergreen forest of relatively mature trees, but you leave that behind and

Clearings in Redden State Forest provide feeding grounds and varied habitats for many reptiles, birds, and mammals.

enter a forest of young loblolly pine, an indication of recent logging. Come upon a T-intersection with another forest road; turn right. The route passes by or through large tracts that have been logged, but the winding way is clear if you stay on the forest road. A couple of old foundations, with trees growing in their centers and with moss-covered bricks now crumbling, can be seen along the right side of the trail. These are believed to be the remains of farmhouses that once stood here.

Come upon a minor cross trail and keep straight. Openings seen along the way are game-food plots. The forest road curves to the right where a minor trail goes left. It curves back to the left at a former boundary corner, identified by a short concrete post marked by peeling yellow paint. This area may be inundated during rainy seasons—and wet enough all year long to support wetlands plants. The going can be difficult, but the mud is full of interesting animal tracks, including red fox. After about 0.5 mile you will once again reach drier ground.

The way curves right where private forestland abuts on the left. Walk by a long, narrow clearing on the right that stretches for about 0.5 mile. Your trail curves right at a big white pine where a minor trail comes in from the left.

Cross Mifflin Ditch on a wooden bridge. Gentians bloom along the edge of the trail in late summer and early autumn. After crossing another stream, pass around a vehicle gate and enter a wildlife sanctuary where hunting is not allowed. Shortly beyond this second stream, turn right on a narrow spur trail through a young loblolly pine forest. It leads in less than 0.25 mile to a T-junction with the wood-chipped Educational Trail at station D. Turn left. The path goes to the office and your waiting vehicle.

Delaware

19. Trap Pond State Park

Around a former millpond in Delaware's oldest state park

Hiking distance: 5 miles
Hiking time: 2.5 hours
Maps: USGS Trap Pond; park map

Trap is one of the most picturesque of Delaware's many millponds. Surrounded for the most part by thick forests, the pond lies in a quiet, rural region. More species of trees are found here than in any other comparable area in Delaware. The tree probably of most interest to visitors is bald cypress, growing profusely along most of the pond's margins and forming a dense swamp near the headwaters. The cypress swamp can be seen best by boat or canoe, but hikers on the trail described here also enjoy fine views. The Trap Pond watershed harbors one of the northernmost stands of bald cypress in the country. Nearly all the original bald cypress forest was cut in the late 1700s. Today, the oldest trees are almost two hundred years old, although most are considerably younger. Some notable specimens approach 5 feet in diameter. Other trees seen along the trail include at least 12 different species of oak (blackjack, black, white, swamp white, red, scarlet, water, willow, Spanish, pin, post, and basket), at least four different species of pine (loblolly, scrub, pitch, and shortleaf), American holly, American chestnut, tulip tree, beech, bigtooth aspen, sweet gum, sour gum, red maple, pignut hickory, persimmon, sweet-bay magnolia, and many others. A multitude of different shrubs and small trees make up the understory. Herbaceous plants are also diverse and numerous; moccasin flower and netted chain fern are two noteworthy examples.

In addition to the varied flora, the hiker has good opportunities to see some of the park's wildlife. Turtles, water snakes, and frogs are common in

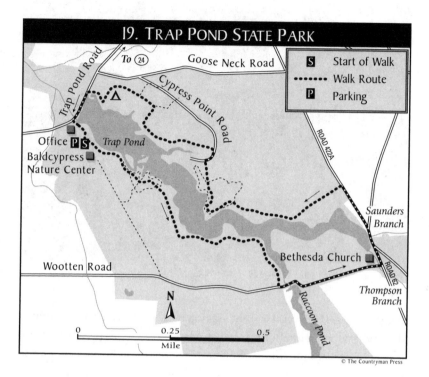

19. TRAP POND STATE PARK

Legend:
- **S** Start of Walk
- •••••• Walk Route
- **P** Parking

and around the pond. Squirrels (both red and eastern gray), eastern chipmunk, eastern cottontail, and other small mammals abound. Typical woodland birds are scarlet tanager, eastern towhee, eastern kingbird, gray catbird, common yellowthroat, wood thrush, northern flicker, and northern bobwhite. Anglers fish Trap for bass, pickerel, bluegill, crappie, catfish, and perch.

The 90-acre pond was created about 1790 to power a gristmill and a sawmill. In 1951, Trap Pond became Delaware's first state park. Your hike circumnavigates the pond on the Boundary Trail in a counterclockwise direction, beginning and ending near the Baldcypress Nature Center. A walk around Trap can be rewarding at any time of the year. In May, swamp

The Boundary Trail passes through deep woods on its five-mile loop around Trap Pond in Trap Pond State Park.

azalea, moccasin flower, and other spring plants are in bloom. Starting in May and extending into June, mountain laurel puts on a spectacular floral display. In the autumn, the earth glitters with leaves of the hardwoods and bald cypress. Flowers of witch hazel burst forth in November. The park is largely deserted by people in the winter, and park roads may be closed to vehicular traffic after snowfalls. However, the trails remain open, and the hiker may see bald cypress locked in ice—an unlikely setting for a cypress swamp. Any remaining open water in the middle of the pond is often crowded with tundra swan, Canada and snow geese, mallard, and American black duck. On sunny winter days, the buckling, shifting ice breaks the silence with deep groans and eerie squeaks that seem to reverberate from shore to shore.

Access

Trap Pond is near Laurel in southern Delaware. From downtown Laurel, head east for 5.3 miles on DE 24, turn right onto Trap Pond Road, and enter the park after 0.9 mile. Continue for another 0.3 mile, crossing the outlet from Trap Pond and then turning left onto the main park road. An entrance fee is charged from May 1 to October 31. After the fee booth, you will come upon a large parking lot. Turn right, drive through the parking area, and enter another large parking lot. Leave your car near the Baldcypress Nature Center.

Trail

From the nature center, walk toward the pond on a wide concrete ramp. Turn right on the Boundary Trail, following a service road through a picnic area with a screened pavilion. Curve right, away from the pond, on the broad Boundary Trail as the narrow Island Nature Trail goes straight. The way borders an athletic field on the right. Just as you enter the woods, the Island Trail loops from the right on its return to the trailhead.

A bridle trail comes in from the right and joins the Boundary Trail. Shortly beyond, you intersect the Island Trail again as it crosses your path. Continue straight, coming upon the primitive youth camping area on the shore. The trail skirts the camping area and stays near the water, affording occasional vistas of the cypress–studded pond.

Slightly more than 0.5 mile from the youth camping area, your trail reaches the headwaters of Trap Pond and turns right gradually, passing a swampy lowland. Bald cypress are mingled with other trees and brush in the swamp. Come out upon paved Wootten Road and turn left.

The road very shortly bridges one of the inlets to Trap Pond. Raccoon Pond is on the right. Hike along the road for slightly more than 0.5 mile, passing by the Bethesda Methodist Episcopal Church. Built in 1878, the small, white, wooden building is no longer used by worshipers. The old church cemetery is pleasantly set beneath tall trees.

Cross Thompson Branch, another inlet to Trap Pond, and immediately come upon a T-junction with paved Road 62. Turn left and cross Saunders Branch. Fork left at the first opportunity onto paved Road 422A. After about 0.3 mile, turn left off the road onto a woods road blocked by posts to prevent vehicular access. A sign here points to the Boundary Trail. Keep straight on the woods road and soon the way becomes canopied by tall evergreen and broad-leaved trees.

Continue on the wide woods road. Keep straight where the narrow Cypress Point Nature Trail crosses your path. The nature trail is soon encountered again as it crosses once more. Continue straight, and you will very soon pass by the disc golf course on the right and come out onto unpaved Cypress Point Road. (To the left, the road soon dead-ends at Cypress Point, where there are picnic grounds and another primitive youth camping area.)

Turn right and follow the road as it curves to the left. Just beyond the curve, turn left off the road onto a broad trail; a Boundary Trail sign points the way. The route joins a utility line and enters the park's cabin camping area.

Continue to follow the utility poles across a parking lot into the campground. Once in the campground, turn right on a wide trail, passing between loop E on the right and loop D on the left. Reach an unpaved campground road and turn left. Walk past the entrances to loops D, C, B, and A on the left and turn left onto the second road into loop A. Go all the way to the end (near the pond) and turn right on a narrow path marked as the Boundary Trail. Bald cypress and buttonbush grow along the pond edge in this vicinity. After about 400 feet, the trail comes out at a boat launch and then turns left onto Trap Pond Road.

The road crosses the dam that impounds Trap Pond. If you are here in spring or early summer, look for barn swallows that frequently nest under the bridge. On the other side of the outlet, descend the steps to the left and follow a sandy service road along the shoreline back to the parking lot. The park office will be on your right, and you will walk past the boat rental building, picnic area and pavilion, and playground before reaching the Baldcypress Nature Center.

20. Wicomico Demonstration Forest

A network of forest lanes and firebreaks through upland woods

Hiking distance: 3 miles
Hiking time: 1.5 hours
Map: USGS Wango

Wicomico Demonstration Forest was created in 1983 from the former Wicomico State Forest. The name change reflected a shift in management emphasis from timber production to a demonstration area for modern forestry practices and an educational training site.

Lumbering still occurs at Wicomico, since tree-cutting is one way to demonstrate scientific forestry and to train modern foresters in the latest techniques. Foresters today learn to manage, not to destroy. Only managed forests are relatively immune from the ravages of old-style slash-and-burn forestry. Best management practices are followed by lumber companies working under contract to the state. Revenue produced by timber sales is used for the operation of the overall Maryland forest system. Foresters now realize that good forest management benefits everyone—forest-product users, hunters, hikers, naturalists, and nature lovers—and serves the good of the land in general. For example, all three of the thrushes that overwinter on the Delmarva Peninsula seem to favor the thick undergrowth of the forest. I saw eastern bluebird, American robin, and hermit thrush during a hike in early February.

A study by forest managers showed that the shotgun deer hunt accounted for 90 percent of the public use of the forest. Other hunters are afield during bow season and small game season. Only an occasional hiker, plant enthusiast, or wildlife observer visits Wicomico during the

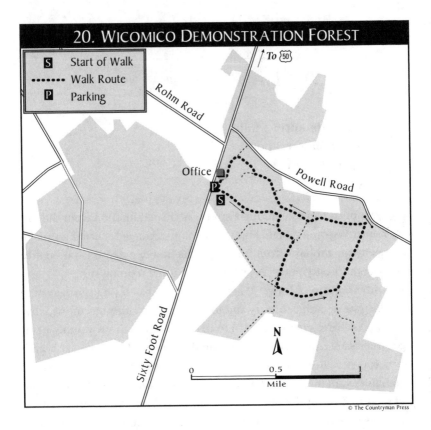

entire rest of the year—the perfect time, then, to schedule your walk. Hunting is prohibited on most Sundays in Maryland. If you are lucky enough to avoid loggers (who usually do not work on weekends), you will likely find a peaceful quietness in the forest, a natural stillness punctuated only by the hum of insects, the call of birds, and the quiet whisper of wind through the loblolly pines.

Access

Wicomico Demonstration Forest is near Parsonsburg. From Salisbury, drive east on US 50 for 9.8 miles to Sixty Foot Road. Turn right. After 1.8 miles, you will come upon the forest office on the left. Turn into the U-shaped drive and leave your car in the small parking area behind the middle building.

Trail

Walk along the drive in the direction of the large, cinder-block garage. Turn left off the drive just before reaching the garage, walk through the grounds, and pick up your trail behind the building. The path to the left is your return route. For now, turn right on the gravel lane. Keep a communications tower and a large yard for old vehicles on your left and soon you will cross a small ditch running along the edge of the maintenance compound. Just beyond, you will come upon a T-intersection; turn left, following the forest lane.

Continue straight on the lane and you will reach another T-junction. Turn right to continue your hike, staying on the broad, main trail. After curving to the left, you will come to yet another T-intersection. Turn right again.

About 1 mile into the hike, you will arrive at a wide cross trail—turn left. Your path reaches a T-junction, with a well-traveled lane entering from the right; turn left here and follow a long straightaway.

The trail is blocked by a gate as it approaches Powell Road. Turn sharply left onto a firebreak just before you reach the gate. The firebreak is much narrower than the very broad forest lanes you have been walking on. Proceed straight on a wide forest lane where a diagonal trail crosses from the right rear to the left front.

Your walk until now has been so remarkably level that you cannot help but notice when you begin climbing a gentle grade through rather deep sand. You are ascending a low hillock—a relic sand dune left behind in the interior of Delmarva after the last ice age caused sea levels to drop between 13,000 and 30,000 years ago. Geologists working in this region

The broad trails in Wicomico Demonstration Forest cross relic sand dunes that may have been formed as recently as 13,000 years ago.

of Maryland first discovered and described the remnant sand ridges; they named the feature the Parsonsburg Sand Formation after the nearby town. Yucca and other plants typical of dry areas are found in this vicinity. Once across the old dune, turn right on a forest lane just before reaching a clearing. A broad trail immediately intersects from the left, but you continue straight.

You will soon come upon a T-intersection; go right on the wide forest lane. Reach a fork in the trail and keep left. Farther along, you will come to another fork; this time, take the right prong, which is narrower and drier. After this second fork you will come to a T-junction. Turn left. The trail soon returns to the headquarters complex by coming out into the big yard that contains old vehicles and the communications tower. Continue straight, following the route behind the buildings until you come upon the drive to the right leading to the parking area.

21. Pocomoke State Forest

A network of wide, level trails in the Pocomoke River watershed

Hiking distance: 3.75 miles
Hiking time: 2 hours
Maps: USGS Snow Hill; forest map

This hike in the Pocomoke State Forest wanders through upland woods and skirts the dense Pocomoke River swamp. The junglelike swamp stretches for 30 miles along both sides of the big, south-flowing river, which arises in Delaware and empties into the Chesapeake Bay. The waterlogged lowlands are 2 miles wide in some places. Naturalist Thomas Nuttall explored the Pocomoke River swamp in 1809. Nuttall, no stranger to difficult terrain and seemingly happiest when he was entering little-known territory, described the swamp as "one of the most frightful labyrinths you can imagine."

Early settlers considered the swamp virtually impenetrable and usually only made forays into it to find the biggest and most valuable bald cypress trees and cut them down. Bald cypress is the noble tree of the swamp, noted for its size and longevity. Bald cypress seldom forms extensive pure stands here near the northern limit of its range, but the trees, with their broadly buttressed and flaring trunks accompanied by protruding root knees, dominate the swamp setting.

In the mid-1800s, the river and its swamps became a link in the Underground Railroad; escaping slaves and their abolitionist guides followed the river north into Delaware and eventually to the relative safety and freedom of Pennsylvania. Some two thousand slaves beat their way north along the "Railroad" on the Eastern Shore. Untold numbers died

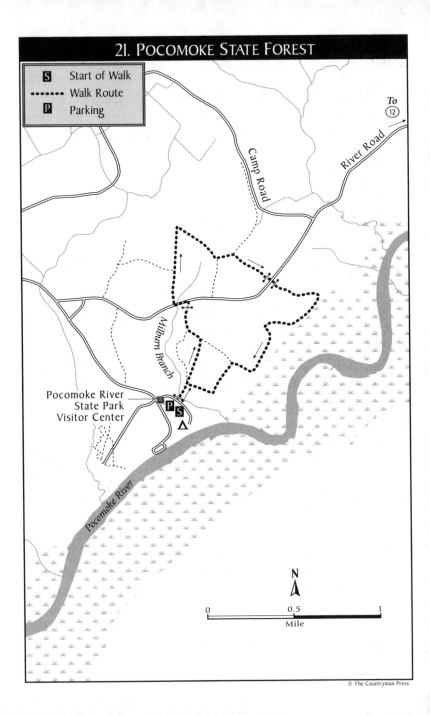

21. POCOMOKE STATE FOREST

S Start of Walk
●●●●● Walk Route
P Parking

To (12)

River Road

Camp Road

Milburn Branch

Pocomoke River
State Park
Visitor Center

P **S**
△

Pocomoke River

N

0   0.5   1
Mile

© The Countryman Press

in the swamps, drowned in the rivers, or were captured by bounty hunters.

During the Civil War, the swamp became notorious as a hideout for smugglers, bootleggers, outlaws, and deserters. After the war, as things returned to normal and technology improved, even the swamp forest became accessible to loggers, and most of the trees were cut down.

The upland areas of what is now Pocomoke State Forest were devoted to agriculture from the days of early settlements until the 1920s. Some of the plowed furrows can still be seen, now lying in thick forests. Diminishing crop yields, depleted soils, and economic hardships forced many people off farms in the 1930s, and the land was abandoned. Government agencies stepped in to set up soil conservation programs and to provide forest fire protection. Maryland began acquiring worn-out farmland and cutover forestland, and the federal government established two Civilian Conservation Corps camps. The old farm fields reverted to pure stands of loblolly pine from natural seeding. Most of Maryland's timber income is derived from loblolly pine, and today the former agricultural lands are providing wood fiber for products such as saw logs, poles, pilings, basket veneer, and pulpwood.

The most obvious signs of the people once living here are the cemeteries they left behind. Scattered through the forest and often victims of neglect and vandalism, the small family burial plots are reminders of the changing patterns of land use. This walk passes by a secluded, 19th century graveyard.

The hike featured here begins in the Milburn Landing Area of Pocomoke River State Park but soon enters Pocomoke State Forest. It follows part of the Milburn Landing Trail through some of the most scenic and interesting parts of the Pocomoke Valley, with good opportunities to see bald cypress in its natural habitat. The way is well maintained and is marked with directional arrows and signs. Chapter 22 describes a shorter hike in the Pocomoke River swamp.

Prepare for this hike with some forethought and careful planning. During certain times, tick and chigger populations reach extremely high levels, and voracious mosquitoes lie in wait at the edge of the swamp. Repellent is *de rigueur* under these conditions. Hunting is allowed throughout the forest. If you are hiking here during hunting season, wear protectively colored clothing. Scheduling your visit to avoid hunting season will add to your safety; hunting on public land on Sundays is prohibited in Maryland.

Access

From downtown Snow Hill, go north on MD 12 for 1.2 miles. Turn left onto Nassawango Road (MD 354 goes right at this intersection). Drive for 2.2 miles, crossing broad Nassawango Creek, and fork left onto River Road where Creek Road goes right. Continue on River Road for 4.3 miles and turn left into Pocomoke River State Park. Drive 0.8 mile along the park entrance road to the first crossroad and turn left, following the signs to the campground. Immediately after turning left, you will see the park visitor center on the right. Park in front of the visitor center.

If coming from Salisbury, drive south on MD 12 for 16 miles, turn right onto Nassawango Road, and follow the above directions.

Trail

Walk down the paved road for 0.1 mile toward the campground, which is open from mid-April to mid-December. A gate prevents vehicular access to the campground during the off-season, but hikers can continue around it. Turn left off the road onto a forest lane, opposite the trailer sanitary station. A small sign here points to "Trail."

The lane descends very slightly to cross Milburn Branch, a little tributary of the Pocomoke River. Here you have your first view of the cypress swamp. Bald cypress lines the waterway downstream of the trail. The strange knees that protrude from the water are thought to deliver oxygen to the root system.

You leave the state park and enter Pocomoke State Forest as you climb out of the miniature valley. Reach a major trail junction. The broad trail to the right is your return loop, but for now you continue straight, walk-

The Bevans family plot in what is now Pocomoke State Forest has gravestones from the early 1800s.

ing up a gentle incline and ignoring another wide trail that leads off the junction at about the 10 o'clock position.

Near the top of the small rise, the old Bevans cemetery is nestled in an overgrown tangle of trees, shrubs, ferns, and greenbriers. The thickets, perhaps aided by vandals, have nudged the weathered, gray tombstones into rakish slants. Other stones in the plot are toppled over, broken off, or leaning against trees. All the graves list burial dates in the first half of the 19th century; the earliest I could find was of Priscilla Bevans, who died April 23, 1828.

Beyond the graveyard, the trail enters a forest of saplings and young trees. Come to a T-junction and turn left. Soon a side trail joins from the left rear. Continue straight to a vehicle gate. Walk around it, pass through a small parking area, and come out onto paved River Road. Turn left (west), cross Milburn Branch a second time, and then turn right (north) on a woods road just beyond a clearing that serves as a game-food plot. You will pass more open food plots scattered through this tract.

The trail reaches the edge of state land after about 0.5 mile, when it nears agricultural fields. Make a sharp turn on the trail to the right rear and stay in the woods. After about 0.25 mile, the Milburn Landing Trail turns left onto a single track where a wide woods road continues straight.

Come to a junction where the Milburn Landing Trail splits; the narrow spur to the left follows an old logging track to the trailhead on Camp Road, and the wider trial to the right continues the loop by following a woods road to River Road and the swamp along the Pocomoke River. Turn right and walk straight in a southeasterly direction for a little over 0.25 mile to reach paved River Road. Cross the road, making your way around vehicle barricades.

South of the road the trail passes through an intermediate-age forest and begins a very gradual descent to the Pocomoke River bottomland. Farther along, the trees are older and are characterized by sweet gum, tulip tree, loblolly pine, and a variety of hickories and oaks. Mountain laurel is prevalent in the shrub layer. After about 0.25 mile, the Milburn Landing Trail curves to the right where it abuts the Pocomoke River swamp and where an overgrown trail comes in from the left. Here you are only about 5 feet above sea level. The Pocomoke River is a tidal river, with up to a 3-foot rise and fall.

Follow the woods road, which keeps to higher ground along the edge of the swamp. At places to the left you can see the steep bank that drops to the bottomland, but the main channel of the river, about 0.4 mile away, is hidden from view by the sheltering wetlands. The suffusive greens of the bald cypress stand out among the red maple, sour gum, and other swamp-loving plants. The trail snakes through the forest, following the contour of the relatively high ground above the river bottom. Pass a side trail forking to the right where your path makes a broad, U-shaped loop around a tongue of swampland. After about 0.75 mile, the way turns sharply to the right, away from the swamp, and soon comes to the edge of an area of younger trees. Turn left on a broad trail where another wide trail continues straight.

The trail turns sharply right at the boundary with Pocomoke River State Park, marked by "No Hunting" signs. Farther along, you will return to the major trail junction seen early in the hike. Turn left, cross Milburn Branch again, and climb to the paved road in the state park. A turn to the right will lead you back to the visitor center.

22. Bald Cypress Nature Trail

A nature walk in Pocomoke River State Park

Hiking distance: 1 mile
Hiking time: 0.75 hour
Maps: USGS Girdletree and Snow Hill; park map

Bald cypress is a southern tree, growing majestically in swampy low-lands of the Atlantic Coastal Plain and along streams and rivers throughout the South. To many people, mature stands of bald cypress draped with Spanish moss represent the primeval nature of the southern swamps.

Although a conifer, bald cypress sheds its leaves in the autumn. It superficially resembles American larch, another deciduous conifer. Maryland is the only state in which both bald cypress and American larch occur naturally. The needles of both turn to a beautiful yellowish brown in the autumn before falling. Both species are typical inhabitants of wetlands, but here their similarities end. American larch, or tamarack, is a northern species, found as far north as the Arctic timberline. In the contiguous United States, it is restricted to cold northern or high mountain bogs where extreme acidity of soil and water permit only certain specialized plants to grow. One such tamarack bog is in the lofty Alleghenies of far western Maryland.

On the other hand, the Maryland populations of bald cypress are found in the southern part of the state. The trees occur sporadically in several bottomland habitats, most notably along the Pocomoke River. The Pocomoke, from its headwaters in Delaware's Cypress Swamp to its mouth at Pocomoke Sound, is lined with bald cypress.

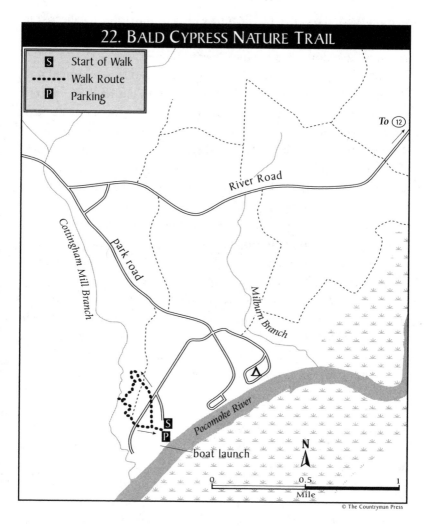

The wood of bald cypress is prized by lumbermen because it is highly resistant to decay. Early settlers along the Pocomoke began logging the swamp and used the cypress for shipbuilding, shingles, siding on homes, water tanks, and coffins. The Pocomoke River swamp forest had been completely logged by the 1930s when the federal and state governments began acquiring abandoned land in the watershed.

With protection, the swamp forest is returning to a more natural state. It will be many years before bald cypress again dominates the swamp; cypress is very slow to regenerate second-growth stands because small trees are shaded by the swamp hardwoods. But it is, after all, the supreme tree of the rich river swamps, and young bald cypresses are making a comeback.

Pocomoke River State Park preserves some of the finest second-growth stands of cypress. The Bald Cypress Nature Trail, in the Milburn Landing Area of the park, brings you to the edge of the cypress swamp, passing through other forest types as well. None of the trees here are wreathed with Spanish moss (that plant drops out in southern Virginia), nor has the cutover cypress forest regained its lofty maturity. Yet the essence of the swamp persists—dark, still, dense, trackless, inscrutable.

This easy walk is well suited for families with young children. Dogs must be on a leash. A leaflet describing the numbered stations along the way is available from rangers or at the trailhead. Bring insect repellent. To see more of the Pocomoke River swamp, take the longer walk through the adjacent Pocomoke State Forest described in chapter 21.

Access

From Snow Hill, drive north on MD 12 for 1.2 miles. Turn left at the flashing caution light onto Nassawango Road (MD 354 goes right at this intersection). Drive for 2.2 miles, crossing the broad Nassawango Creek, and fork left onto River Road where Creek Road goes right. Continue on River Road for 4.3 miles and turn left into Pocomoke River State Park. Follow the entrance road for 0.8 mile to the first crossroad and turn right, following the sign to the boat ramp. Proceed 0.4 mile and then turn left onto a side road. Reach the parking lot for the boat ramp after 0.1 mile and park on the right, at the trailhead for the Bald Cypress Nature Trail.

If coming from Salisbury, drive southeast on MD 12 for 16.1 miles, turn right onto Nassawango Road, and then follow the above directions.

Thin wisps of autumn mist rise at dawn from the Pocomoke River in Pocomoke River State Park. The 73-mile-long Pocomoke was the first Maryland river to be designated as wild and scenic.

Trail

The way begins in a mixed hardwood forest of maples, tulip tree, sweet gum, oaks, and other species. A few loblolly and scrub pines also grow along the path. After station 3, fork right; you will return to this spot along the left fork.

Beyond station 8, pass over a shallow ditch on a wooden bridge. Walk diagonally across a paved park road and reenter the forest.

The path ahead goes straight at a cross trail and tunnels through a dark thicket of mountain laurel. It shortly reaches the Pocomoke River swamp and your first trailside view of cypress trees. The characteristic bald cypress knees that stick out of the water are believed to deliver oxygen to the root system. The path curves around the edge of the bottomland for about 0.25 mile. In late summer and autumn, the rich humus along the edge of the swamp is a good place to find Indian-pipe and pinesap, small saprophytic plants of the wintergreen family that lack chlorophyll.

A short spur leads from the main trail along an old road to an observation deck overlooking Cottingham Mill Branch (also called Cottingham Mill Run). This creek, convoluted and choked with chaotic plant growth, is representative of the myriad small waterways that course through the swamp.

Go back to the main trail, turn right, and continue walking along the swamp margin. Cross a wooden bridge over a slough between stations 21 and 22. Beyond station 22, the Bald Cypress Nature Trail leaves the swamp behind and turns right sharply on a broad trail where another wide trail goes left and a narrow path continues straight.

Past station 23, you will come out into an open area. Walk straight across the paved park road and reenter the woods. After station 25, veer right on the entrance spur that leads back to the parking area.

23. Kiptopeke State Park

Beetles, butterflies, and birds along the Chesapeake Bay

Hiking distance: 1.6 miles
Hiking time: 1 hour
Maps: USGS Townsend; park map

Chesapeake means "great shellfish bay" in the original indigenous language. Through the ages, many shamans, sages, poets, philosophers, and other writers have discoursed enthusiastically on the Chesapeake. An early settler described it as "the Noblest Bay in the Universe." H. L. Mencken called it a "great big outdoor protein factory."

The bay's grandeur, quiet beauty, fecundity, and life-sustaining qualities place it prominently on the list of earth's superlatives. It is 195 miles long, 3 to 35 miles wide, and has 11,600 miles of shoreline. It is North America's largest and most productive estuary and one of the largest and most productive estuarine systems in the world. The Chesapeake is obviously of immense economic importance to Virginia, Maryland, and neighboring coastal states because of its fishing and recreational value, but it is also absolutely essential to the multitudes of wildlife that live all or part of their lives in the water or on the shore. The bay is the spawning, nursery, or feeding grounds for one hundred species of fish. Well over half a million waterfowl can be found overwintering each year on the Chesapeake. Ospreys are more common around the bay than anywhere else in the United States, and bald eagles nest along its shore.

Kiptopeke State Park is a good place to experience the simple benefits that the Chesapeake provides and to learn about the ecological and economic importance of the bay. Hiking, camping, canoeing and kayaking,

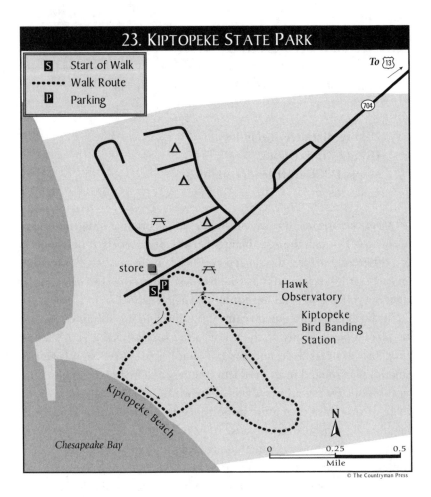

wildlife observation, picnicking, swimming, fishing, and crabbing are some of the activities available in the 540-acre park, which includes about 1 mile of bay beach. The state runs interpretive and naturalist programs from Memorial Day weekend to Labor Day, along with hawk observatory and bird banding station programs in September and October. The

U.S. Environmental Protection Agency cooperates with the park to stage environmental education workshops. Kiptopeke State Park is one of the centers for the Eastern Shore Birding Festival, held every year on the weekend following the first Wednesday in October.

The state park occupies land that once served as a terminal for ferries operating between Cape Charles and Virginia Beach. A couple of the old terminal facilities, dating from the late 1940s and early 1950s, are still standing. The former ferry dock is now a lighted fishing pier open 24 hours a day. Nine World War II ships were grounded offshore to serve as a breakwater for the terminal; they are now a nesting area for gulls and an artificial reef for fish. Ferry service was discontinued in 1964 with the opening of the Chesapeake Bay Bridge-Tunnel.

The bay, sandy beaches, maritime forests, dunes, bayberry thickets, and old fields are abundant with avian life. The waters adjacent to the park teem with marine creatures, such as tiny scuds less than 0.125 inch long, big Atlantic blue crab over 7 inches across, prize black drum that tip the scales at more than 80 pounds, and the "most celebrated of American turtles," the seldom seen diamondback terrapin.

This hike is ideal for families with children, especially during warm days of the fall migration. There are good opportunities to search for shells on the beach, to see beach plum in fruit, and to watch little birds being handled and studied. You may have a chance to release a bird to the sky after it has been banded. To top off a perfect walk, there is a playground near the end. Dogs are welcome in Virginia state parks, but they must be on a leash.

Access

From the center of Eastville, drive south on US Business 13 for 1.3 miles to US 13, then continue south for another 11.3 miles to VA 704. Turn right and go 0.5 mile to the park. An entrance fee applies. Continue straight after the contact station for 1.1 miles and park near the gray-boarded camp store at the head of a big parking lot on the waterfront.

Trail

The Wood Warbler Walkway, a boardwalk through a maritime forest, starts opposite the store. The way leads through a tangled growth of loblolly pine, scrub pine, sassafras, American holly, Atlantic red cedar, northern bayberry, and greenbriers. The trail's name is appropriate. All of the wooded and brushy areas of Kiptopeke offer good chances to see warblers during migration; the elevated boardwalk, which puts you at eye level with the tops of the low-growing trees, affords excellent, up-close views of these small, colorful songbirds. Migrating monarch butterflies also often fly through the scrubby forest.

Soon you reach a side trail to the left that descends by steps to the Baywoods Trail. Continue straight on the boardwalk and reach Kiptopeke Beach along the Chesapeake Bay after about 0.2 mile. Descend to the beach and turn left. Walk on the hard, compacted sand near the water to avoid disturbing the northeastern beach tiger beetle, a federally endangered species that lives and hunts in the soft sands above the tide line. Once common along much of the Atlantic coast from here north to New England, the beetle has suffered a drastic decline in population because of habitat destruction. Virginia is the southern limit of the beetle's range, and Kiptopeke Beach is one of only about forty localities where the beetle is still found.

The view from the shore is almost always filled with action. The distance directly across the Chesapeake to Marsh Point on Plum Tree Island National Wildlife Refuge is about 15 miles. Watermen may be out on the bay in their boats, laying or retrieving their nets or working their trotlines. Watch for ospreys that patrol the quiet cove and dive to snatch fish in their talons. Far out on the water you can see the Chesapeake Bay Bridge-Tunnel, the 17.6-mile-long engineering marvel across the mouth of the Chesapeake that caused the ferry service to shut down and that ultimately led to the formation of the state park. Take time also to look closely at your immediate surroundings. If you are lucky, you may spot one of the colorful tiger beetles scurrying about the upper beach in pursuit of smaller

A boardwalk on Kiptopeke State Park's Wood Warbler Walkway bridges sand dunes to reach curving Kiptopeke Beach on the Chesapeake Bay.

insects. The sand at your feet is marked with the tracks of little crabs that scavenge the tide line and then retreat into their burrows.

After about 0.25 mile, come to another boardwalk—the Peregrine Passage Walkway—and turn left. The curving beach ahead of you is closed to protect critical habitat for the northeastern beach tiger beetle.

The Peregrine Passage Walkway climbs steps to cross the dunes. After entering the forest, the way reaches a T-junction with the Baywoods Trail. Turn right. The trail is wide, level, sandy, and well-marked as it goes through a forest of loblolly pine and other trees. The path curves to the left when it reaches a farm field; after a short distance it turns left again to reenter the woods.

Come to the Kiptopeke Bird Banding Station. If you are here during the fall migratory season (generally from September through November) you will see staff members and volunteers of the Coastal Virginia Wildlife Observatory operating long baffles of fine-mesh mist nets to capture and band songbirds. After quickly recording information on species, weight, and other conditions and attaching a small band to a leg, they release the birds to continue their journey. Birds have been banded at Kiptopeke since 1963—it is one of the longest-running migratory banding stations in eastern North America. The skein of data collected by researchers and observers at Kiptopeke and at nearby Eastern Shore of Virginia National Wildlife Refuge (see chapter 31) provides a valuable portrait of the migratory patterns of songbirds along the Atlantic coast.

After the bird banding station, the wide Baywoods Trail turns left and passes by a butterfly garden maintained by the Coastal Virginia Wildlife Observatory. A stop here may allow you to see resident and migratory insects, including predatory species like mantids that lie in wait to capture butterflies.

Keep more or less straight on a narrow trail past the butterfly garden. You soon reach a cross trail; turn right toward the Hawk Observatory. This is a wooden, handicap-accessible, elevated platform that offers unobstructed views of the horizon. If you are here during fall migratory season you will see observers with notebooks and binoculars, using standardized methods to spot and record raptors as they fly over. Started in 1977, the annual watch typically counts in excess of seventy thousand birds of prey. The Coastal Virginia Wildlife Observatory reports that Kiptopeke State Park is the best place in the world to see migrating peregrine falcon and merlin.

The Baywoods Trail curves left and a side path goes right in the vicinity of the Hawk Observatory, but you leave the park's trail network and walk through the adjacent picnic area, which has restrooms, drinking water, and a playground. Continue to a small parking area and follow a paved lane as it descends to the main park road and the big lot where you parked your car.

Delaware Bay/Atlantic Ocean

Assateague Island

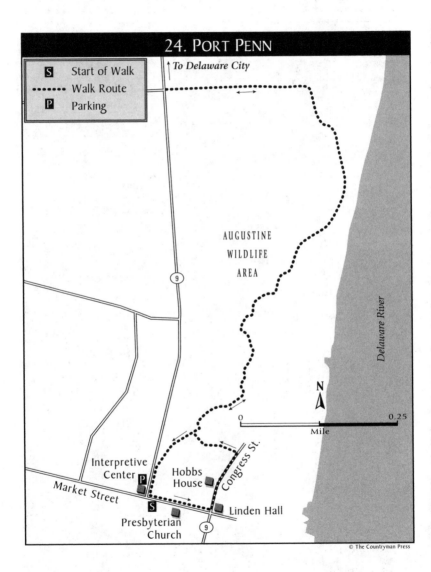

24. PORT PENN

- **S** Start of Walk
- **•••••** Walk Route
- **P** Parking

↑ *To Delaware City*

AUGUSTINE
WILDLIFE
AREA

Delaware River

N

0 — 0.25
Mile

Interpretive
Center **P**

Market Street

S

Hobbs
House

Congress St.

Linden Hall

Presbyterian
Church

© The Countryman Press

24. Port Penn

A stroll through an old river town and out into the marsh

Hiking distance: 2 miles
Hiking time: 1.5 hours
Map: USGS Delaware City

After an almost two-month voyage across the North Atlantic on board the 300-ton *Welcome*, William Penn rounded the Delaware Capes on his 38th birthday and came ashore at a small wharf connected to a bit of fast land along the Delaware River. He came to America to accept possession of his New World holdings granted to him by England's King Charles II. First he stopped here to get a drink of fresh water. That was in October 1682. The place, which had been sparsely peopled with Dutch and English settlers for about 40 years, has been known ever since as Port Penn.

Port Penn gradually coalesced into a populated area and became a town in 1694. It was not until around 1750 that Port Penn was formally laid out. David Stewart, a physician and town planner, created a design of streets and lots at right angles with a central market square, similar in style to other upriver cities like New Castle, Wilmington, and Philadelphia.

Surrounded on three sides by water, Port Penn grew steadily and slowly into a small market town oriented toward the river and its tidal marshes. Port Penners worked on the waterfront, labored in the surrounding farm fields, or performed tasks such as carpentry or blacksmithing for the maritime and agricultural economies. The townspeople benefited from the natural cycle of the river, netting American shad and Atlantic herring in the spring, fishing for Atlantic sturgeon in the summer, hunting waterfowl in the autumn, and trapping muskrat in the winter.

The Delaware produced more shad than any other river on the East Coast. In 1896, some 15 million pounds of shad were caught along the Delaware. Sturgeon harvests were counted in the hundreds of thousands; today the state of Delaware lists Atlantic sturgeon as an endangered species. Market gunners used big "punt guns" to shoot migratory waterfowl without limits, bringing down a large number of birds in one sprayed shot. In the early 1900s, some ten thousand muskrats were trapped in one winter in a single marsh near Port Penn.

Around the turn of the 20th century, the village and nearby Augustine Beach were destinations of pleasure boats from big upriver cities. Picnic grounds, bathhouses, summer cottages, church camps, and fishing piers sprouted along the banks.

The 20th century also brought the first hints of drastic change for the worse on the Delaware, as the long years of use and abuse caught up with the village, the marshes, and the river. By the 1920s, the Delaware had grown so polluted that the American shad fishery collapsed. The museum in town includes a quote from an old waterman who remembered, "I've seen a man put in his net [during the 1920s] and come out with not one fish. Not a one." Huge refineries, power plants, and other industries replaced the shad processing sheds. Coastal storms of 1930 and 1950 damaged the shoreline and caused widespread flooding. Overfishing, overhunting, increased population, wetlands destruction, water pollution, erosion, siltation, and industrialization all contributed toward the environmental decline of the bay. Bruce Stutz quoted a longtime waterfowl hunter in 1992:

> They started dredging and filling the marshes, and in a few years all the duck hunting and the rail bird shooting, all the excitement come September—it was like you turned off a switch. Guys quit gunnin' and sold their boats, put their decoys away . . . beautiful decoys . . . Delaware River decoys, hollowed out and the feathers carved out and not just painted on. When the wood got a little low in the fireplace, he'd just toss a decoy in there.

The Delaware began to lose its value as a natural refuge and as a haven for the culture—places like Port Penn—it once shaped. Now, however, at the turn of the 21st century, the river is seeing improvements in water quality and habitat. In its wetlands, the river still retains a good deal of its natural inheritance. Many species of fish are beginning to return. In the 1970s the Delaware Department of Natural Resources and Environmental Control established wildlife areas in the marshes north and south of Port Penn. The village itself is the scene of efforts by the state and the Port Penn Area Historical Society to honor the long history of the townsfolk and preserve their traditional activities of fishing, trapping, and hunting.

The state runs the Port Penn Interpretive Center and has set up exhibit signs along a walking tour of the village. The walk is linked to an interpretive trail that wanders through part of the Augustine Wildlife Area north of town.

The hike described here follows village sidewalks to see some of the historic buildings. You can explore further by taking side streets. All the houses in Port Penn are private and not open to the public. The walk then leaves the village and strikes out onto the Augustine Wildlife Area through the woods and fields and then across the marsh on a long dike.

Take time to visit the Port Penn Interpretive Center before you hike. It is a mood-rich museum that traces the 360-plus years of Port Penn history. The center and the walk through the village and marsh will help you gain "a sense of the landscape as it shapes the lives of the people who call it home, just as the people mark the land," as Southwest author Diana Kappel-Smith wrote. "Each defines the other," she observed.

Booklets describing numbered stations along the way are available at the Interpretive Center, which is open Friday through Sunday from Memorial Day weekend through the last weekend of September. Part of the trail goes through a public hunting area, so exercise caution during hunting seasons. Hunting is not allowed on Sundays in Delaware.

At sunset, spindly trees etch the sky in 2,630-acre Augustine Wildlife Area on the Delaware River.

Access

Port Penn is on DE 9 about 4 miles south of Delaware City. The Port Penn Interpretive Center is at the northwest corner of DE 9 (Liberty Street) and Market Street. Parking is available behind the center, off DE 9.

Trail

The Port Penn Interpretive Center is housed in a two-room schoolhouse built in 1886. Grades 1–10 were taught here until around the middle of the 20th century, when it was converted for use for grades 1–6 only. The school closed in 1961, when the student body had fallen to 12 pupils. The Delaware Division of Parks and Recreation acquired the old building in 1991 and today uses it to showcase the town's cultural and natural history.

Port Penn never achieved the prominence hoped for by David Stewart. The result is a quiet river hamlet that appears today much as it did in the past. Begin the Village Walk in front of the Interpretive Center, facing

Market Street. The empty lot across the street is the site of the former cannery where the famous Port Penn tomatoes were canned.

Turn left and cross Liberty Street. Walk along Market Street one block to Stewart Street and the Presbyterian Church. The brick house of worship with the tall wooden steeple was built in 1856. The lot on the corner opposite the church is the old Market Square.

Continue on Market Street to the next intersection (Congress Street). The timeworn building on the northeast corner is Linden Hall. This brick mansion was built on the riverfront in 1845 by Joseph Cleaver, a rich merchant and trader, during the heyday of Port Penn's prosperity. It is still the largest house in town and is undergoing renovation by the state of Delaware.

Leave Market Street by turning left on Congress Street. Near the edge of town note the Hobbs House, a Sears & Roebuck mail order house, on the left. You reach the edge of town very quickly after the Hobbs House. Continue on the road as it enters the marsh. After about 0.1 mile you will see a sign indicating that you are entering the headquarters complex for the Augustine and C&D Canal Wildlife Areas.

Walk along the road for about another 0.25 mile; woods border the road on the left, and on the right is a tidal marsh characterized by an almost pure stand of common reed (*Phragmites*). Towering as high as 15 feet, this supple plant that rustles with the slightest breeze is supported by a network of underground rhizomes or rootstalks, which store nutrients and give the plant a head start each growing season. Common reed usually turns green and begins sprouting early in the spring, before other plants begin leafing out. The creeping rhizomes can extend a stand of reeds by as much as 30 feet a year. This invasive native plant now fills 40,000 acres of brackish marsh along the Delaware River and Delaware Bay. Common reed crowds out cattail and other marsh plants. When it takes over, birds such as least bittern, king rail, moorhen, and marsh wren lose the cattails they need for nesting. The dense reed canopy leaves fewer spots for turtles to bask, and the accumulated mat of dead reed litter prevents other plant seeds from reaching the marsh soil to germinate. Marshes choked with reeds lack muskrats, which do not feed on common reed, and also rice rats and voles that share muskrat lodges. The tall, feathery reeds can be considered one of the reasons for the decline in habitats along the Delaware—another in a long line of events that led to the demise of a way of life attuned to the river.

A field begins on the left after the woods end. Ahead you will see a mowed grass area around a stone house. Turn left off the road and follow the edge of the field on the left and the grass on the right. The way leads back to a mowed trail that continues for a short distance to a T-junction. You will return to this spot later, but for now turn right. You are following the Port Penn Wetlands Trail in the Augustine Wildlife Area.

The trail comes out onto a paved turnaround. An arrow on a post directs you across the pavement and out onto a dike to your left. The dike is blocked by a vehicular gate that you can easily walk around.

Walk north on the dike. Structures like this had their beginnings in the mid-1600s when Dutch farmers set up water control projects in an attempt to drain the marsh and plant crops. Their experience in the low country of Holland helped them in the engineering of the New World dikes. A 1950 hurricane destroyed the dike, but it was rebuilt to keep floodwaters off DE 9.

A channel controlled by a tide gate runs under the dike. Just beyond is an observation platform. My last journey to Port Penn was on a cloudless, late summer day. It was not long to the equinox, and the sun was setting nearly due west. The marsh was deserted but for a great blue heron, standing motionless in the shallow water, only its feathers ruffling in the wind. The heat of the afternoon was giving way to the chill dampness of the marsh at evening. Crickets skirled from the weeds along the dike. Near the tide gate, I found a small family band of Latin American immigrants who had walked in and stopped here to fish and eat. Children ran and played games. Women sat and talked, keeping an eye on the kids while tending a small fire. Men cast their nets and lines in the marsh and the channel. Although they might not know it, they were carrying on the tradition of scores of previous generations of marsh dwellers, including Native Americans, who sought their food and their fun in the water. The family epitomized the Port Penners described in one of the town exhibits: "They knew the marsh like an old friend. They considered the marsh both companion and provider, asking of it a simple living."

The Port Penn Wetlands Trail ends at the observation platform, but why stop here? The path ahead beckons, and you can continue north on the dike for more views of the teeming marsh. Some of Delaware's most productive wetlands, perhaps as productive as any tropical rain forest, are tidal areas such as this.

The trail makes a 90-degree turn to the left and goes out to DE 9, opposite the intersection with Thorntown Road. From this juncture, you can turn left and walk along the highway about 0.75 mile to town, but the road is narrow and busy. Find a more pleasant way by turning around and walking back through the marsh.

Return past the observation platform, the tide gate, the paved turnaround, all the way to where the grassy path comes in from the left. From this point, keep walking straight on the Port Penn Wetlands Trail. The way leads across a long boardwalk and passes by exhibits of a muskrat skinning shack and a fisherman's floating cabin. The trail comes out onto DE 9 across from the Port Penn Interpretive Center.

25. Blackbird State Forest

An upland forest walk featuring Delmarva bays

Hiking distance: 3 miles
Hiking time: 1.5 hours
Map: USGS Clayton

Blackbird State Forest consists of nine separate tracts in north-central Delaware. The Tybout Tract, with over 1,000 acres, is the setting for this hike. Many areas of the Tybout Tract are former cultivated fields replanted with pines. These groves of evergreens, now tall and stately, provide striking contrasts with the climax deciduous forest found on other portions of the state land. "Each pine is like a great green feather stuck in the ground," as Henry David Thoreau wrote in an 1851 entry in his *Journal*.

This region is noted for the sharply defined circular or elliptical depressions scattered throughout the flat terrain. To a hiker attuned to changes in landforms and to subtle differences in vegetation, these oval lowlands command immediate attention; they are clearly unlike their surroundings. Sometimes called Carolina bays because of superficial similarities to other depressions first discovered and described in the Carolinas, these sinks may be as much as 20 feet below the encircling rim (although most are considerably shallower). Those in this area are more appropriately called Delmarva bays to distinguish them from those in the South.

The depressions are spectacular in a quiet sort of way. Much of their appeal lies in their unique biota and in their scattered but regular occurrence in small geographic areas. Their origin has defied explanation and remains a mystery. Lorraine Fleming, in *Delaware's Outstanding Natural Areas and Their Preservation,* points out the special character of these puzzling landforms:

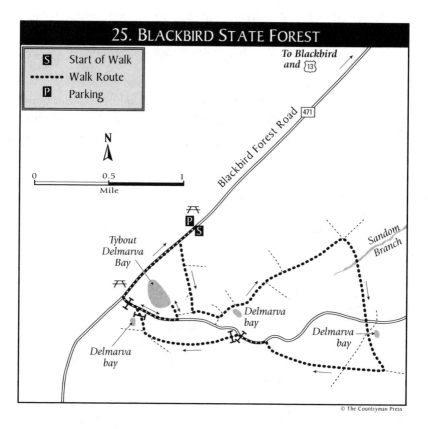

25. BLACKBIRD STATE FOREST

S	Start of Walk
•••••••	Walk Route
P	Parking

To Blackbird and [13]

Blackbird Forest Road [471]

Sandom Branch

N

0   0.5   1
Mile

P **S**

Tybout Delmarva Bay

Delmarva bay

Delmarva bay

Delmarva bay

© The Countryman Press

The origin of [Delmarva] bays, also termed sinkholes, whale wallows, round ponds, black bottoms, and loblollies, is a subject of considerable controversy. A number of theories have been advanced, but not one has been adequately substantiated or widely accepted. An intriguing but implausible idea contends that whales were stranded by shallow receding seas and wallowed helplessly, thus creating the depressions. Others include ancient meteorite impact, the melting of stranded ice debris originating from Pleistocene glaciation, and the "water table-sinkhole-lacustrine-aeolian" theory, a two-phase geomorphic cycle in which a basin phase is followed by a bay phase and finally drainage by stream incursion. [Delmarva] bays are in every sense of the word geological and biological enigmas.

Thousands of Delmarva bays punctuate the coastal plain in this part of Delaware and neighboring Maryland, all occurring within a 50-mile radius and generally running in a diagonal southwest-northeast band. Most have been altered or destroyed by ditching, draining, cultivation, filling, or development. The few undisturbed bays remaining are usually the deeper ones found in wooded areas. Recognized as unique natural treasures containing wet meadow and swamp plant communities found nowhere else in the country, the unaltered bays are now receiving protection. In 1984 Delaware established the Blackbird Carolina Bays Nature Preserve within Blackbird State Forest to conserve the bays and their immediate surroundings. The Nature Conservancy and the Maryland Department of Natural Resources have protected and restored many outstanding bays in the Old Line State.

This hike passes by some fine examples of Delmarva bays, nestled among trees and now protected from man-made changes. You may also see some altered bays in adjacent agricultural fields. Delmarva bays are poorly drained and may contain water throughout the year; thus, most hikers view them from the perimeter. They can perhaps be seen best in late autumn or winter, when the water may be absent or at least lowered and when the leaves are off the dense vegetation; ice-covered bays are strikingly scenic. The rich plant communities of the Delmarva bays—the abundant grasses, sedges, and wildflowers—reach the peak of their beauty in late summer and early autumn.

Trees along this walk include scrub pine, white pine, loblolly pine, red pine, tulip tree, sweet gum, black tupelo, white oak, willow oak, swamp white oak, flowering dogwood, red maple, persimmon, and several hickories.

Most of the trail lies within a public hunting area. I recommend you visit at a time other than firearm deer season, usually scattered days from October to January. Call the forest office at 302-653-6505 if you are planning to hike during those months. Hunting is not allowed on Sundays in Delaware.

Access

From Wilmington, drive south on US 13 for 26.9 miles to the little community of Blackbird. Turn right on Blackbird Forest Road (Road 471). Enter Blackbird State Forest after 1.6 miles. In another 0.5 mile you will see a small picnic area on the right (the first picnic grounds on the right after entering the forest). Park in the picnic area lot.

Trail

Cross Blackbird Forest Road and turn right. Walk along the road for a short distance and turn left off the road through a break in the hedgerow. This leads immediately to a trail junction, with paths going straight, left, and right. Choose the wide way straight ahead. The trail passes through a young forest of mixed hardwoods and conifers. The trees on the right— predominantly tulip tree and sweet gum—are part of a hardwood regeneration project started after the timber was clearcut in 1984. The forest on the left is an evergreen plantation seeded in 1946–47 with white, red, and loblolly pines to serve as a forest demonstration area.

Keep right where a side trail comes in from the left out of the pines. The hardwood regeneration area is left behind and the path wanders through an imposing grove of tall white pines. Keep left at a fork in the trail. Reach a T-intersection as you come out of the pines. Turn left, walking on a broad path between a coniferous forest on your left and a deciduous forest on your right. Your trail angles near a one-lane forest road but turns sharply left where a short side trail, blocked by a cable, goes right to intercept the road. You will see other parts of this one-lane forest road later in the hike.

After about 0.5 mile, you will come upon another trail going both left and right. Turn right and immediately cross over a cable strung between two posts. Just beyond, you will enter a narrow forest road. Turn right. The small tear-shaped lowland visible to the right during all these turns is a Delmarva bay.

The forest road very soon turns sharply to the left, leaving the Delmarva bay behind. The road separates a white pine plantation (planted in 1960) on the left from hardwoods on the right. Continue on the road where a trail

Winter ice locks the Tybout Delmarva Bay, one of several curious, elliptically-shaped wetlands in Blackbird State Forest. The unusual landforms in the forest record Earth's puzzling geologic history and earned it designation as a nature preserve in 1984.

goes off to the right and, beyond, where a forest road leads left to the ranger station and office. Tall, spindly loblolly pines, also planted in 1960, replace the white pines in the plantation on the left.

Where the loblolly pine plantation ends, you will come upon a cross trail. Turn right, descend very slightly, and cross Sandom Branch on wooden bridges. Beyond the stream, the broad path climbs gently and passes through mature oaks and hickories in a secluded section of the forest. I found the old skull of a red fox at the base of a willow oak near the trail.

Cross diagonally the one-lane forest road you saw early in the hike. Just beyond the road, pass a cross trail and continue straight. Close to this intersection is a small, shallow Delmarva bay on the left. Keep left at a fork where a short trail leads right to a deer stand.

Continue straight to a T-junction with a boundary trail that runs along the border of state land. Turn right and follow the narrow swath marked by horizontal yellow blazes on trees. Farm fields come into view on the left as a side trail enters from the right. After the harvest, when the fields lie fallow, you can see elliptical low areas in the farmland—remnants of Delmarva bays drained for agriculture. Woodchucks are common in this area; their burrows are just inside the trees at the edge of the field.

Continue straight at a cross trail. After slightly more than 0.5 mile following the border of state land, your trail angles right and soon intersects the one-lane forest road at a T-junction. Turn left and walk a short distance along the road.

Pass through a metal gate on the road and enter a turnaround and small parking area. The road, wider now, leaves the turnaround at about the 2 o'clock position, but you take a trail at about 10 o'clock, blocked by a cable slung between a tree and a wooden post.

Your trail again brushes the forest boundary. Continue straight whenever you encounter side trails to the left or right. Your path curves right when it reaches a small Delmarva bay. Keep the lowland on your left and soon again reach the one-lane forest road at a cable barricade and a small parking lot.

To reach the Tybout Delmarva Bay, the largest in the immediate vicinity, turn right on the road and walk about 0.1 mile around the bend. A small area for parking one or two vehicles will come into view on the left. The bay can be reached by bushwhacking a short distance through the forest at the back of the parking lot. Descend slightly to the left and arrive at the edge of the depression. The Tybout Bay covers about 1 acre, and the water is about 4 feet deep in the center. Sphagnum moss forms a thick, spongy layer around most of the perimeter. Lichen-encrusted persimmons occur farther in, with dense tangles of buttonbush near the middle. This bay is one of seven making up the Blackbird Carolina Bays Nature Preserve.

To continue, make your way back to the forest road and turn right. This route shortly leads to paved Blackbird Forest Road. Get around the vehicle barricade, cross the road, turn right, walk past a picnic area, and after about 0.3 mile you will arrive back at the small picnic area where you parked your car.

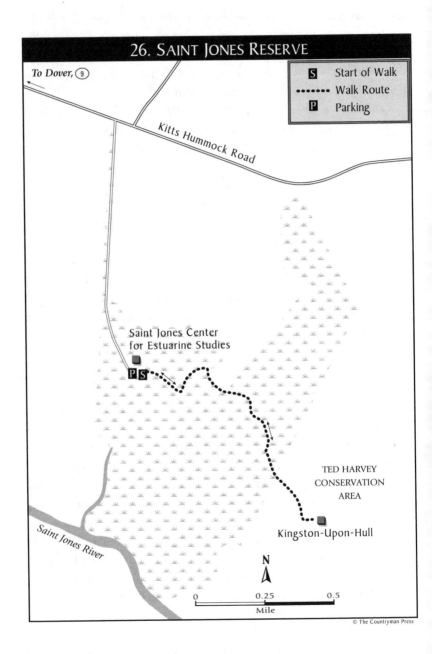

26. SAINT JONES RESERVE

To Dover, (9)

S	Start of Walk
•••••••	Walk Route
P	Parking

Kitts Hummock Road

Saint Jones Center
for Estuarine Studies

P S

TED HARVEY
CONSERVATION
AREA

Kingston-Upon-Hull

Saint Jones River

N

0	0.25	0.5
Mile

© The Countryman Press

26. Saint Jones Reserve

Easy walking along a superlative estuary of national significance

Hiking distance: 2 miles
Hiking time: 1 hour
Map: USGS Frederica

The Saint Jones Reserve is the larger of the two components that make up the Delaware National Estuarine Research Reserve. Its nearly 700 acres protect the tidal marshes, wetlands, and uplands near the mouth of the Saint Jones River on the Delaware Bay. The exceptional features of the lower Saint Jones were recognized by the National Oceanic and Atmospheric Administration, which, in partnership with the Delaware Department of Natural Resources and Environmental Control, established the reserve in 1993. It is one of 26 estuarine ecosystem sites in the country and one of only two on the Delmarva Peninsula (the other is on the Maryland shore of the Chesapeake Bay).

Estuaries are where fresh water meets and mixes with the salt water of the sea and where water levels are affected by tides. The result is a distinctive aquatic environment, a place that is very different chemically, physically, and biologically from both freshwater and saltwater habitats. The Saint Jones Reserve features a relatively small estuary (the Saint Jones River) that is part of a very big estuary (the Delaware Bay)—an arm of the North Atlantic Ocean.

Estuaries are noted for their extraordinary richness and diversity of life. They straddle an ecological boundary between river and bay, between terrestrial and aquatic systems. Scientists have found them to be among the most productive natural places on earth. Climate and location make the Saint Jones estuary home to a stunningly rich and

A boardwalk in Saint Jones Reserve arrows across a salt marsh and carries the Saint Jones River Trail to a ragged row of scraggly trees on dry land.

varied flora and fauna, ranging from microscopic diatoms and zoo-plankton, through vascular plants such as saltmarsh cordgrass, to top-of-the-food-chain predators like coyote and great horned owl.

The Saint Jones Center for Estuarine Studies near the trailhead has interesting exhibits and displays on the natural history of the area. The center helps meet one of the main goals of the reserve—to educate the public on how the waters of rivers and estuaries are inseparable from the life and quality of the Delaware Bay and why it is important to protect wild areas like the Saint Jones River. A stop at the building before your walk will help you understand the biology and history of the estuary, including the intricate life patterns of its plant and animal communities and the ecological balances that sustain them. You can also pick up a printed guide keyed to numbered stations along the hiking trail.

Another major goal of the reserve—research—is represented by the laboratories and monitoring stations housed in the building and along the trail. Scientists and students use the sanctuary as a field station to study the complex ecological relationships occurring in estuarine systems.

Your walk is on the easy-to-follow Saint Jones River Trail through the salt marsh and surrounding areas. Mosquitoes are plentiful, so repellent is needed. The Saint Jones Reserve is open weekdays (except holidays) from 8 to 4:30 and on Saturdays (except holidays) from 10 to 2. It is closed on Sundays. If the entrance drive is gated, you can park in a small lot and walk in along the gravel road. It is about 1 mile to the trailhead (about 2 miles roundtrip). The trail is open to hikers daily from sunrise to sunset. Part of the trail is in the Ted Harvey Conservation Area, a public hunting site. This stretch of the route is closed some days during hunting season. Call the center at 302-739-3436 to plan your hike. Hunting is not permitted on Sundays in Delaware.

Access

Follow US 113 south from Dover for 4.7 miles to the junction with DE 9. Turn left (north) and go only 0.1 mile to an intersection with four-way stop signs. DE 9 turns left at this crossing, but continue straight on Kitts Hummock Road, traveling down Saint Jones Neck. After 0.7 mile, turn right into the Saint Jones Reserve. Follow the gravel entrance road about 1 mile to the parking lot at the Saint Jones Center for Estuarine Studies.

Trail

The Saint Jones River Trail leaves the parking lot to the right of the center. Exhibit signs and numbered posts along the trail are designed to inform the hiker about estuaries and how human activities impact them. One of the most interesting displays is the center's tertiary septic system at the trailhead.

The path enters a small woods but soon emerges to cross a long boardwalk above the tidal marsh that lines the Saint Jones River. The trail never reaches the main channel, but the true nature of the lower river can be gleaned from the extensive marsh seen from the trail. A solar-powered weather station, a sampling station, and a short dock along the boardwalk show that the reserve is indeed a working research center.

The trail leaves the boardwalk and follows a wide hedgerow. Farm fields are on the left and the salt marsh stretches off to the right.

Leave the hedgerow and cross a reedy marsh on a high boardwalk. If you are here in the leafless months, look for American mistletoe growing high in the branches of some of the trees near the boardwalk. The trail reenters the woods and soon crosses a utility line right-of-way. The route enters the Ted Harvey Conservation Area past the utility line and may be closed during hunting season. The pathway is clear and broadens beyond the right-of-way. Keep straight on the double track and ignore some narrow side trails that lead to deer stands.

The forest begins to thin and the trail skirts a scrubby old field on the left. The isolated ruins of Kingston-Upon-Hull sit on a low knoll at the edge of the field. The two-story, brick-and-wood house was built in the late 1600s or early 1700s.

The Saint Jones River Trail ends at Kingston-Upon-Hull. Turn and walk a mile back to the center.

27. Killens Pond State Park

Around an old millpond on the Murderkill River

Hiking distance: 2.75 miles
Hiking time: 1.5 hours
Maps: USGS Harrington; park map

Killens Pond presents a study in contrasts. It lies in the midst of rich farmland and consequently shares the fate of most bodies of water subject to agricultural runoff. Erosion from farmland not only clogs the streams that feed Killens but also fills the pond with sediment, increases turbidity, and contributes to pollution from pesticides, fertilizers, and animal wastes that permeate the silt load. Of all these assaults, excessive nitrate pollution from fertilizers and animal wastes is probably of chief concern because of its potential hazard to human health. The persistently high nitrate levels in Killens Pond led the state of Delaware to close the public beach and build a concrete pool with chlorinated water for swimmers. (The pool has been expanded to include two spiraling water slides, interactive water features, and an area for toddlers and infants.)

On the bright side, the pond still serves as a focal point for recreation and for the plants and animals that depend upon it for sustenance, shelter, and breeding habitats. Fishermen prize the largemouth bass, pickerel, crappie, and bluegill they pull from Killens. River otters hunt and play in its waters. Red foxes prowl the pondside thickets and upland fields. Raccoons search the shoreline and the shallows for food and raise their young in the hollow trees of the surrounding forest. Ring-billed gulls usually can be seen soaring over the open water. In the winter, large numbers of tundra swans use the pond as an overnight resting place. A true sense of wildness can be experienced by standing on the shore on a February

27. KILLENS POND STATE PARK

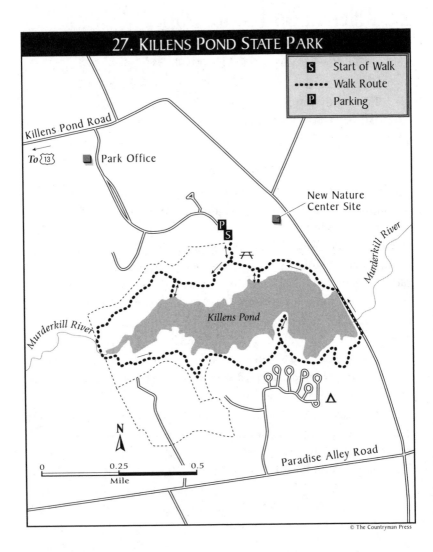

S Start of Walk
•••••• Walk Route
P Parking

Killens Pond Road

To 13

Park Office

New Nature
Center Site

Murderkill River

Killens Pond

Murderkill River

N

0   0.25   0.5
Mile

Paradise Alley Road

© The Countryman Press

evening and watching these great white birds, with wingspreads up to 7 feet, descend from the sky. Occasional pairs arrive at first, followed by small groups of six to eight birds, then larger flocks of 15 to 20. Each arrival is occasion for high-pitched, amiable chattering among all the swans. Soon the darkening waters are filled with a resonant uproar that reverberates from shore to shore. The spectacle is repeated at daybreak. A few birds take flight at first light while others leave later in larger groups. Once airborne, these flocks usually circle the pond to gain altitude and to get into flying formation, cooing all the while, before heading out to feed in the fields and marshes.

The plant community surrounding the pond also will delight the hiker at any season. Most noticeable are the tall trees, especially tulip tree, oaks, and loblolly pine. A few of the park's latter species are infested with fungi or viruses that cause the needles to grow in thick, tufted clumps on some of the high branches. Such irregularities are called witches' brooms because of their fanciful similarities to sinister supernatural objects.

In late winter and early spring, the low-lying areas along the trail brighten with the large green leaves of skunk cabbage. Later in the year, lady's slippers grace the forest floor and flowering dogwoods add splashes of white to the understory.

Killens was originally a millpond made by damming the Murderkill River; the old gristmill is no longer in evidence. Today the 66-acre pond is a natural area in central Delaware. The Pondside Nature Trail featured in this hike (totaling 2.75 miles) circles the pond in a counterclockwise direction, mostly through a mixed deciduous-coniferous forest. A short segment is along a paved road. Numbered posts along the way correspond to entries in a trail leaflet available from park rangers.

Access

Killens Pond State Park is located near Felton. To reach our trailhead, go south from Dover on US 13 for 10.8 miles. Turn left onto Killens Pond Road and travel 1.2 miles to the park entrance on the right. An entrance

Winter snow cloaks American holly and other trees on the Pondside Trail in Killens Pond State Park, near Delaware's geographical center.

fee is charged from May 1 to October 31. Go 0.7 mile to the end of the park road and leave your car at the rear of the large parking lot, near the telephone and bulletin board. Picnic areas with pavilions are also in this vicinity.

Trail

The entrance spur to the Pondside Nature Trail is at the middle back of the parking area. Walk through a beautiful mixed deciduous-coniferous forest of loblolly pine, tulip tree, American holly, and white oak. As you top a small rise, Killens Pond comes into view at a T-junction. You will return to this spot later, but for now turn right onto the Pondside Nature Trail and start your hike around the pond.

The path skirts magnificent stands of American holly (the state tree of Delaware) that grow profusely along the swampy margins of the pond.

Giant loblolly pine and tulip tree are found on drier ground overlooking the water. There are pleasing views of the pond from most stretches of the trail, but be sure to also follow the short side trails to the left that lead to the water's edge or to overlooks for even more expansive vistas. The first such opportunity occurs beyond station 3. The side trail leads to benches on the shoreline.

The Pondside Trail joins an abandoned road in the vicinity of station 7 and passes over low ground to cross the slow-flowing Murderkill River on a long, wooden bridge. Your pathway leaves the old road on the far side of the bridge and, entering a less-developed portion of the park, curves left to stay close to the water. Here at the upper reaches of the pond is an ideal place to stop for a few minutes and catch sight of some of the birds inhabiting this area. A belted kingfisher may come rattling by, or you may spot a great blue heron stalking fish in the shallows. Song sparrows are common in the shrubs that line the banks, and barred owls frequent the tall trees at twilight.

The trail edges the shore, crossing sluggish inlets and swampy areas on short bridges or long, winding boardwalks. The nature trail reaches the park's primitive youth camp and passes through the cabin area. The pathway is well marked in this vicinity.

Beyond station 15, the nature trail turns right where a side trail goes left a short distance to a high, wooded promontory—a good place to enjoy sunrises and sunsets. In the winter, watch for tiny bands of Carolina chickadee and tufted titmouse darting from tree to tree. Return to the Pondside Trail and soon reach the park's campground. At station 16, a cross trail leads right uphill to the campground or left down steps to a small wooden pier.

After climbing into and out of a ravine, the trail descends to a parking area and a boat launch. Walk out to Killens Pond Road and turn left. Cross the dam on the Murderkill River and leave the road by turning left through a break in a post-and-rail fence. Walk through a grassy area with a few picnic tables and benches. Pass by the watercraft rental concession building.

The route broadens at the top of a small rise. A side trail to the right leads to the water park. Soon you reach a trail to the left that goes down to the pond and station 21. A thickly forested shore, a picturesque cove, and a little island in the pond make this an especially attractive spot. Back on the Pondside Trail, a short walk will take you to the entrance spur and a return to your waiting car.

28. Prime Hook National Wildlife Refuge

History and wildlife in the marshes bordering Delaware Bay

Hiking distance: 3.5 miles
Hiking time: 2 hours
Maps: USGS Lewes and Milton

This hike features a lot of variety in a short distance. Beginning in upland fields bordered by wild roses and studded with warty-barked trees, the trail goes by a 19th-century cemetery before reaching a boardwalk into a marsh. The path then loops back through a wooded swamp. Next, a spur takes you down a dike beside a narrow waterway opening into an expansive marsh, a great sea of reeds and grasses dotted with a few forested hummocks. Finally you loop through farm fields and woodlots.

Bombay Hook and Prime Hook became the only national wildlife refuges in Delaware in 1998 when Congress passed the National Wildlife Refuge Improvement Act, which did away with the Killcohook National Wildlife Refuge. Bombay Hook is larger, but Prime Hook is a better place to hike and, with over 9,700 acres, still has excellent opportunities at any season for observing mammals, birds, and other wildlife. Because Prime Hook is primarily a migratory refuge, spring and autumn are especially good times to view waterfowl here. During these seasons, tens of thousands of birds use the refuge as a resting and feeding area during their migrations along the Atlantic flyway. The normally quiet ponds and creeks become crowded with noisy concentrations of ducks and geese. Peak periods vary depending on the weather, but generally the few days around March 15 and November 1 are best for witnessing this age-old pageant-in-the-sky.

Prime Hook is designated as a Wetlands of International Importance under the Ramsar Convention—one of only 17 sites in the United States. The first trail you will hike—the Boardwalk Trail—was built by the Youth Conservation Corps in 1973 and renovated in 2001 to make it accessible to people in wheelchairs.

Access

From Georgetown, head east on US 9 for 5.8 miles. Turn left (north) on DE 5 and drive 5.0 miles to Milton. There turn right (east) on DE 16 and go 3.8 miles to Turkle Pond Road. Turn left and enter the refuge in only 0.1 mile. Continue on the refuge road for 1.4 miles until it dead-ends into the parking lot at the refuge office and visitor center.

Trail

The Boardwalk Trail begins as a small-graveled path on the north side of the parking lot. The way soon passes by the old Morris family burying ground on the left. The Morris estate once stood near this spot but was torn down around 1968. The cemetery is remarkably well preserved, thanks to the protection it receives from the federal government. Most burials date from the mid-1800s. The inscription on one weathered gray stone, barely decipherable after all these years, offers some grim advice to hikers and others who walk this way:

> *Behold ye stranger that pass by*
> *As you are now so once was I*
> *As I am now so must you be*
> *Prepare for death and follow me.*

Beyond the graveyard, the trail leaves fast land and goes out upon the edges of Shell Beach Pond by means of a boardwalk. Fine views of the marsh that covers most of the refuge can be enjoyed from the boardwalk.

You soon loop back to solid ground and pass through a small forest. This area becomes a wooded swamp, and another boardwalk keeps the trail above water. The way turns sharply right, crosses a small ditch, and

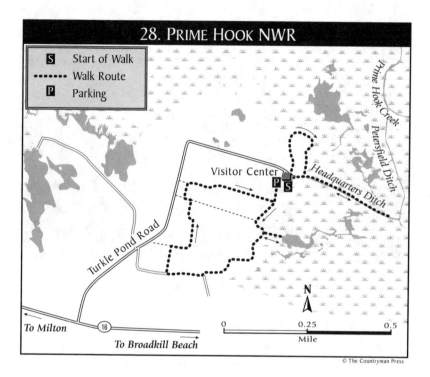

28. PRIME HOOK NWR

S Start of Walk
••••••• Walk Route
P Parking

Visitor Center

Headquarters Ditch

Prime Hook Creek

Petersfield Ditch

Turkle Pond Road

N

To Milton

To Broadkill Beach

16

0   0.25   0.5
Mile

© The Countryman Press

enters an open field. Watch for woodchuck burrows hidden in the grass. The trail turns left and leads through an opening in a hedgerow to climb slightly to the Dike Trail. Turn left.

The Dike Trail parallels Headquarters Ditch, a man-made channel allowing boat access from the refuge office to Prime Hook Creek, which courses through the marsh. A few forested clumps along the trail and in the midst of the marsh indicate the small, sandy hummocks, a few feet higher than the rest of the terrain and consequently drier. Many of these little islands of trees are known to have served as temporary camps for Indians who came to the marsh to fish, hunt, and gather shellfish and crabs.

Hikers on the Black Farm Trail in Prime Hook National Wildlife Refuge find a visual feast at the edge of a vast tidal marsh bordering the Delaware Bay.

Bird life is abundant here. The tree-covered hummocks provide shelter for many birds not normally encountered in marshland. Owls roost in the branches, using the woody islands as a base for their nighttime forays. Northern flicker, red-bellied woodpecker, northern mockingbird, and warblers fly about. Out on the open marsh you will likely see red-winged blackbirds flitting along the ditch, vultures circling overhead, gulls soaring by, and perhaps a northern harrier sailing low over the tall reeds in its unmistakable, buoyant hunting flight. Waterfowl abound during migrations.

Walk about 0.5 mile to a wheelchair-accessible observation platform at the end of the Dike Trail. Headquarters Ditch meets Petersfield Ditch in a T-intersection at this spot. Turn around and hike straight back the Dike Trail to the parking area.

Continue through the parking area and around the headquarters and visitor center complex, keeping the buildings on your left. Behind the fenced motor pool you will find the trailhead for the Black Farm

Trail, a very wide, mowed track that begins at the edge of an old field and a small woodlot. The trees are soon left behind and you walk through fields.

As you approach a wooded area of mostly Atlantic white cedar, you reach a cross trail. You will return to this spot later along the right trail, but for now continue straight into the forest, still walking on a broad, mowed swath. Beyond the forest, you come upon another cross trail. Turn left. (The way to the right is a shortcut on the Black Farm Trail.) Shortly after this junction, a short side path leads left to a beautiful spot overlooking the marsh.

Back on the main trail, the route passes over a culvert connecting low areas on either side. American mistletoe grows on the trees in this vicinity. The bottomland is soon left behind and the trail passes through old fields. After crossing a hedgerow, you will see an agricultural field on the right. Farmers grow crops on the federal land under the Cooperative Lease Program, planting soybeans or corn in the spring and reaping their harvest in the fall. In late autumn, they plant the fields in winter wheat to be used by geese as browse during the cold months.

Walk through a hedgerow and turn sharply right on a double-track farm lane. An agricultural field is on the right and an old field, overgrown with grasses, multiflora rose, and small shrubs, is on the left.

Turn off the double track onto a broad, mowed swath. An old field is still on your left and the farm field is on your right. Directional trail signs are posted at most of these turns.

Reach a T-junction at the edge of a forest. Turn right, keeping the woods on your left. A couple of mowed firebreaks enter the woodlot, but keep walking along the edge of field and forest. The way curves left at a 90-degree turn. The boundary between the woods and the fields is a good place to look for raptors such as red-tailed hawk.

You come to a hedgerow with a cross trail. Turn left and walk along the hedgerow for about 400 feet. Then turn right into the woods in an area characterized again by Atlantic white cedar. If you continued straight, you would reach a trailhead parking lot on Turkle Pond Road.

Cross over a low area on the Bill Baumgardner Bridge and reach a T-junction at the edge of the woods. Turn right and follow the edge between the woods and the field. The way may be wet in places, but the terrain rises slightly and the muddy areas are left behind. Reach the spot you encountered before on the Black Farm Trail. A turn to the left will lead you back to the visitor center parking lot.

29. Cape Henlopen State Park

The essence of Delmarva: bay shore, ocean beach, sand dunes, forest, pond, bogs, and salt marsh, complete with abundant wildlife and compelling human history

Hiking distance: 9.25 miles
Hiking time: 4.5 hours
Maps: USGS Cape Henlopen; park map

Cape Henlopen was identified on Spanish maps of the New World as early as 1544. The English navigator Henry Hudson, sailing under the Dutch flag in 1609, found a snug haven behind the cape for his ship the *Half Moon* and claimed the area for Holland. Dutch settlers arrived in 1631, but the colony was annihilated by Indians. A second colonization, in 1658, was successful.

The cape is one of present-day Delaware's most prominent landmarks, a kinetic peninsula jutting boldly from the land. The Atlantic surf pounds the eastern shore. Waves and wind constantly chisel and hew the shoreline into new shapes and forms, inexorably resculpting the cape's profile. On the west, by contrast, lies a quiet harbor where gentle waves allow the sand to settle and accumulate and thus add to the measure of the land.

Since Cape Henlopen is a landscape in flux, it is exquisitely beautiful and endlessly fascinating. In spite of the harsh and rapidly changing environment, the plant and animal communities of the shore are fragile and remarkably diverse. The beach itself is home to an array of living things, usually augmented by whatever the sea casts up. The dunes, the most unstable of the cape's environments, nevertheless are often covered with beach grass, beach heather, broom sedge, and switchgrass. The more stable parts

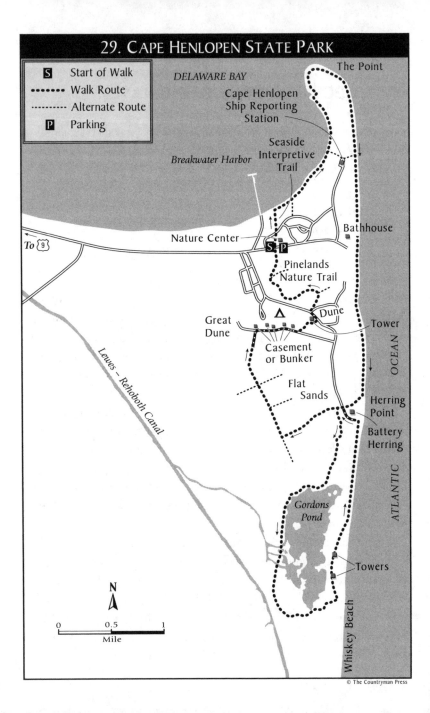

29. CAPE HENLOPEN STATE PARK

S Start of Walk
••••• Walk Route
------ Alternate Route
P Parking

DELAWARE BAY

The Point

Cape Henlopen
Ship Reporting
Station

Seaside
Interpretive
Trail

Breakwater Harbor

Bathhouse

Nature Center

To 9

S **P**

Pinelands
Nature Trail

Dune

△

Great
Dune

Casement
or Bunker

Tower

OCEAN

Lewes – Rehoboth Canal

Flat
Sands

Herring Point

Battery
Herring

ATLANTIC

*Gordons
Pond*

Towers

Whiskey Beach

N

0   0.5   1
Mile

© The Countryman Press

of the cape support mature forests of pine, oak, cherry, cedar, and a host of smaller associated shrubs such as highbush blueberry and sassafras. Interspersed in the woodlands are small bogs rich in sundews and large cranberry. The salt marshes behind the dunes and the forests are densely covered with salt hay, salt-marsh cordgrass, groundsel tree, and common reed.

White-tailed deer roam the woodlands. Northern bobwhite abound both on the dunes and in the forests; in summer opportunities prevail to see family broods—mother, father, and their host of chicks. Seabirds and shorebirds are abundant. Mosquitoes and deerflies are common, too, especially off the beach, so repellent is suggested for this walk.

Cape Henlopen is the site of a former military installation, one of the key posts in this country's coastal defense network during World War II. The military lands have been turned into a state park—Delaware's and Delmarva's largest.

The walk recommended here can be hiked in its entirety only in October, February, and a few weeks in November, December, and January. Some stretches of bay shore and ocean beach are closed to all visitors from March 1 to October 1 to protect rare nesting and migrating shorebirds. Some interior trails are closed for about one week each in November, December, and January for the shotgun deer hunt. Hunting is prohibited in Delaware on Sundays. Stretches of trail near Gordons Pond may become flooded during periods of high water. Call the park office at 302-645-8983 or the park's Seaside Nature Center at 302-645-6852 to check on current conditions as you plan your hike. Dogs on leash are allowed on some trail segments, but not on others, so it is better to leave your dog at home.

This hike follows parts of both nature trails in the park. Hikes along the entire lengths of these trails provide additional walks that are enjoyable and educational. Brochures describing the trails are available from the Seaside Nature Center or from rangers. Please read the section on beach walking in the introduction of this book before hiking the cape.

Access

From Georgetown, go east on US 9 for 17 miles to Cape Henlopen State Park. An entrance fee is charged from May 1 to October 31. Once inside the park, continue straight for 0.3 mile to the Seaside Nature Center on the left. Park your car in the center's lot.

Trail

Walk around to the left of the nature center and begin your hike on the Seaside Interpretive Trail. Numbered stations are keyed to the descriptive pamphlet explaining items of interest along the path. The trail winds through the low dunes. Black rat snakes frequent the thickets, foraging for lizards, toads, and small birds and mammals. Their sinuous tracks can often be seen along open, sandy stretches of the path.

After about 0.25 mile, the trail comes out onto the beach of Breakwater Harbor, a broad cove of the Delaware Bay. A long fishing pier is to the left, and a lighthouse stands on the stone breakwater that guards the harbor. Turn right on the Seaside Trail and walk along the beach.

The bay shore is almost always a scene of activity. Shorebirds, terns, and gulls search the beach and the shallow water for food. Various forms of marine life have been cast onto the beach: common oyster, mussels, slipper shells, razor clams, and Atlantic horseshoe crab are abundant. The Delaware Bay is renowned for its large populations of horseshoe crabs. At times, it is almost impossible to walk this trail without stepping on them or their skeletons. Tens of thousands of horseshoe crabs come shoreward during high spring tides to mate in the shallows and to lay their eggs on the beach. Thousands die when they become stranded, their skeletons forming a low, ragged wall at the high-tide mark.

The Seaside Interpretive Trail turns right at station 11 and reenters the sand dunes. Continue straight, along the shore. Come upon a dune crossing walkway. The rolling dunes, lying in the heart of the cape, serve as an important shorebird and seabird breeding habitat. Piping plover, black skimmer, and least and common terns nest here. Piping plover is the most imperiled of these species; it is listed as threatened by the federal govern-

An idyllic spot on the Atlantic shore, Herring Point in Cape Henlopen State Park provides a respite from the more demanding manmade attractions of nearby coastal resorts.

ment and endangered by the state. Cape Henlopen is the only place in Delaware where the piping plover nests. The beach is also used by the young fledglings and by migrating shorebirds. No entry is permitted north of the dune crossing walkway during nesting and migrating season (March 1 to October 1). If you are here during those times, you can continue the hike by taking the dune crossing walkway to the ocean beach and turning right (south).

The short, thick tower in the dunes is the Cape Henlopen Ship Reporting Station, operated by the Philadelphia Maritime Exchange and the Delaware Bay Pilots Association. Observers in the tower monitor ship traffic moving in and out of the Delaware Bay, dispatch navigational pilots to incoming vessels, and notify port operators up the bay of ship arrivals.

After the dune crossing walkway and the tower, the shore begins angling northward toward the point of Cape Henlopen. Follow the shoreline, noting the long tongues of sand and mud that extend into the harbor. These accreted spits of land, best seen at low tide, have been formed by sediments carried by the erosional forces of wind and water from the seaward side of the cape. They are present-day evidence of the erosion and migration of the cape that has been occurring for at least the last eleven thousand years. Geologists describe the spread of the sea over land areas and the consequent sedimentation on older deposits as transgression. Additional transgression will eventually enable these spits to gain height and length and be transformed into dunes far removed from the migrating shoreline. Later, your trail crosses some larger, ancient recurved spit tips that had their origin as small sand bars on the bay side of old Cape Henlopen. They are now thickly forested and are located about 1.5 miles inland to the south.

At the point, where the land, bay, and ocean meet, you will come out onto a very broad expanse of open beach, broken only occasionally by small, isolated clumps of vegetation. A lighthouse sits on a breakwater off the coast and guides mariners to safety with both a beacon and a horn. Fully automated, it replaced the original Cape Henlopen lighthouse erected in 1765. The old lighthouse, built on land and victim of the eroding shoreline, fell to the sea in 1926.

Curve to the right, turning south in a gradual arc, and walk along the Atlantic Ocean. You will reach a dune crossing walkway that connects with the bay shore. This is the alternate trail that you would have taken during nesting and migrating season. You will also see the Cape Henlopen Ship Reporting Station from the ocean side, but keep your eyes on the sea in this vicinity. If you see an inbound freighter, you may be able to spot the little boat dispatched by the station that comes alongside the big ship and drops off the pilot.

After almost a mile from the point, you will enter a surf fishing area, with dune crossings for both foot travelers and off-road vehicles. Continue south for about another mile to the life-guarded swimming area, with telephone, bathhouse, water, and food available in season. The northernmost dune crossing walkway at the swimming beach is the eastern end of the transcontinental American Discovery Trail. From here it goes west to the Pacific Ocean, arriving at Point Reyes, California, after 4,678 miles. It is the country's longest trail.

South of the swimming area, the headland to the west overlooking the sea is the Great Dune, also called Sand Hill. Rising to about 90 feet above sea level, it is the highest point along the North Atlantic between Massachusetts and North Carolina. Military strategists recognized the importance of this high land near the mouth of the Delaware Bay and built a fort. The old concrete bunkers and observation towers, part of the coastal defenses during World War II, still stand on the Great Dune and at other nearby places. Like nearly everything else at Cape Henlopen, the Great Dune is not static; it is slowly migrating south.

As you continue south, you will come upon a dune crossing for vehicles and hikers; go straight, staying on the beach. Some small, stunted scrub pines grow on the front dune. Many have died from the harsh conditions dealt by the salt spray and wind, but others are holding on. A ghost forest—a few battered tree stumps awash in the surf—attests to the slow, westward erosion of the beach and the ultimate fate of the trees on the dune.

Reach Herring Point, marked by a long groin of boulders jutting into the sea. Just south of the groin (an effort to stabilize beach erosion), turn right off the beach onto a walkway that leads through the dunes. Climb the steps to a parking area. Battery Herring—a former naval gun emplacement built in 1942—is behind a fence directly across the lot. There are picnic tables on the point, along with magnificent views of the ocean and the beach below. This is also a good place to observe birds; during my last visit, two bald eagles soared over, almost at eye level. Leave Herring Point by the gradually descending paved road at the back of the parking lot.

At the bottom, reach a main road that goes left to a vehicle dune crossing and right to the developed portions of the park. You will return to this spot later, but for now continue straight across the road and enter a wide lane blocked by wooden posts. Soon after you leave the road, and just before you enter a forest of rather large loblolly pines, turn left on a narrow path.

The trail entrance is marked by a brown post, and occasionally there are other brown posts along the way. The path leads through a beautiful, remote section of the park, scrambling up and down sand dunes and wandering through scraggly forests of pitch pine. Views of the distant ocean can be had from the crest of some of the higher dunes.

The route leaves the dunes and drops down a steep, sandy face into a pine flat. The trail widens as it approaches Gordons Pond and skirts a marshy shoreline. Some stretches may be underwater during wet seasons, so be prepared to either wade or turn around. The pond, marsh, and surrounding mudflats are excellent places for wildlife observation. Great egret, greater yellowlegs, American black duck, northern harrier, white-tailed deer, muskrat, and a great variety of butterflies are common here.

The trail passes over an inlet on a corrugated metal bridge and then traverses a dike between the pond and a salt marsh. Reach the junction with the Bike and Pedestrian Trail (also called the Gordons Pond Trail). An observation platform at this intersection has exhibit signs on migratory birds and provides a scenic overlook of Gordons Pond and the surrounding marsh. The high-rises of Rehoboth Beach can also be seen. Go left on the graveled Bike and Pedestrian Trail.

The way passes close to the Lewes-Rehoboth Canal. After about 0.75 mile, the trail becomes paved and reaches a parking lot at the southern end of the state park. Turn left off of the trail, cross a road, and enter the parking lot. Walk toward the left (north) edge of the parking area, keeping most of the parking spaces on your right, and head straight for a dune crossing walkway. Go through the dunes, reach Whiskey Beach, and turn left (north) along the ocean.

Pass two World War II–era U.S. Army Coast Artillery observation towers, awash in the surf. The towers were of course not built in the water when they were erected in 1942—they were placed far back in the dunes. The fact that they are now at the edge of land is dramatic evidence of the slow, westward migration of the shoreline under the onslaught of the sea. Another cape structure—the lighthouse near the point—lasted over a hundred years before being claimed by the waves.

It will be interesting to see if these concrete towers are still standing in the 2040s.

The beach in this area is closed to protect nesting piping plover and other shorebirds from March 1 to around the middle of August. There is no alternative route; if you reach this area during nesting season, you must turn around and retrace your steps.

When you again come to Herring Point, you will find a dune crossing walkway adjacent to an off-road vehicle crossing on the south side of the point. Follow the dune crossing walkway, which joins the vehicle road at the back of the dune. Old Battery Herring is visible on the right, at the top of the dune. Return to where the paved road leads down from the Herring Point parking lot and turn left into the wide lane. Now, instead of turning left onto the trail that leads to Gordons Pond, continue straight on the lane into a forested region known as the Flat Sands. Bracken forms dense stands in the understory, while loblolly pine is the predominant tree. The trails in this area are closed during shotgun deer season, usually three separate weeks in November, December, and January.

About 0.5 mile from the road, you will come upon a broad cross trail (an old military road) at a T-junction; turn right (northwest). A few side trails will be encountered, but continue straight for almost a mile as the old road crosses low, sandy, densely forested ridges alternating with marshland. These ridges are the recurved spit tips mentioned earlier. They are the relics of old Cape Henlopen, deposits of sand and gravel formerly near the cape's point and left behind in ancient times by wind and waves. The marshes represent remnants of a shallow lagoon, much like today's Breakwater Harbor, that remained unsilted during the cape evolution. Your trail bisects the narrow tongues of sandy ridge and salt marsh, which resemble the interlocking fingers of folded hands upon the landscape. Old shells have been used to raise the route above the waters of the marsh, but expect wet conditions nevertheless.

The old military road reaches a major trail intersection. A kiosk has a map showing the Walking Dune Hiking Trail network, and spur trails lead left to a marsh observation post and right to return to the paved road. To continue your walk, keep straight.

Your trail becomes paved with asphalt as it passes a cinder-block building on the right. Continue straight on the pavement, walking by a fenced enclosure on the right containing atmospheric monitoring equipment, part of the University of Delaware's acid precipitation research program. Come upon a T-intersection with a paved lane at the south face of the Great Dune. The way to the left leads in 0.25 mile to a dune overlook. Turn right to continue your walk. A former ammunition storage casemate, mostly buried in the side of the dune, is seen at the junction.

The paved lane climbs very gradually past other ammunition storage casemates. The park campground sits atop the Great Dune, above the old bunkers. Immediately after the fourth ammunition storage casemate, and only about 0.25 mile from the T-junction, the route forks. Yogi Berra said, "If you see a fork in the road, take it." This time, take the paved left fork (called the Tower Spur) and climb slightly.

Reach a T-junction. A former Army Coast Artillery observation tower is on the left, at the crest of the Great Dune. This silo-like tower and others like it at Cape Henlopen were used during World War II as observation posts to spot enemy vessels and to direct the fire of the shore batteries. A turn to the right here continues your hike, but take time to go left a few steps and climb the tower, the only one in the park that is open. You will have the same view as did the soldiers on alert during the war. The coast is clear today, but the threat was real in the 1940s. German U-boats sank thousands of tons of shipping off the Delaware shore in 1942 alone. War's end saw one of the two most deadly U-boats surrender and strike her colors at Lewes.

Back on the trail, you shortly reach a paved road. Jog left across the road and immediately turn right into a parking lot. At the back of the parking lot, to the left of a low, cement-block building, is the entrance to the Pinelands Nature Trail—Delaware's first national recreation trail (designated in 1981). Leave the parking lot and enter the pinewoods.

Shortly reach a T-junction. The Pinelands Trail goes both left and right, but your choice is to turn left and follow the trail down the numbered stations (11, 10, 9, etc.) keyed to the booklet that describes the human and natural history of the pinelands. The way is easy to follow through an open loblolly pine forest. It passes by a relic bog, still remaining despite repeated attempts to ditch and drain the wetlands of the cape to reduce mosquito breeding places.

The trail splits at station 5. Go left and follow the spur toward the nature center. Come out of the woods into the Parade Field. Cross the old military parade grounds and road to reach the Seaside Nature Center.

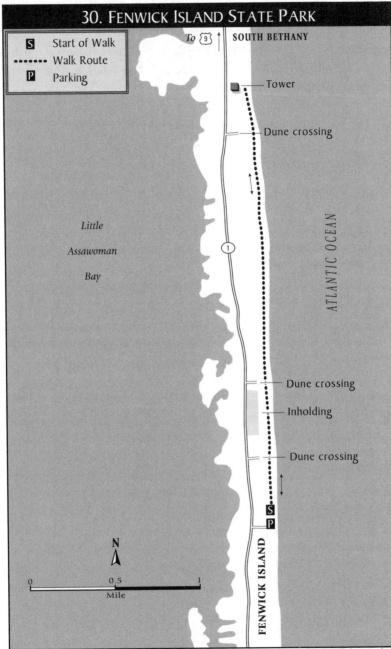

30. FENWICK ISLAND STATE PARK

To 9   SOUTH BETHANY

S   Start of Walk

•••••••   Walk Route

P   Parking

Tower

Dune crossing

Little

Assawoman

Bay

1

ATLANTIC OCEAN

Dune crossing

Inholding

Dune crossing

S

P

N

0   0.5   1
Mile

FENWICK ISLAND

© The Countryman Press

30. Fenwick Island State Park

Beach walking in Delaware's southeastern corner

Hiking distance: 5 miles
Hiking time: 2.5 hours
Maps: USGS Assawoman Bay and Bethany Beach

Fenwick Island State Park is an oasis of open space along the Atlantic Ocean in extreme southeastern Delaware. It is a welcome refuge amid the oceanfront developments that stretch nearly fifteen miles from Ocean City, Maryland, to Bethany Beach, Delaware. Here you can experience what Oliver Wendell Holmes in "The Chambered Nautilus" called the "unresting sea." The North Atlantic beats relentlessly, sometimes with short, steep breakers, sometimes sweeping with thunderous rhythm onto the shore with long, widely spaced swells that may have come all the way from Portugal. The park features a wide ocean beach of clean sand and rolling surf backed by a system of low dunes. Boat-tailed grackle, black skimmer, several species of gulls and terns, and various shorebirds frequent the sunstruck beach. I have seen pods of up to 20 dolphins swimming and cavorting in the ocean less than 200 yards from shore.

Fenwick Island is not an island at all but rather a long, narrow bar extending southward from its connection with the mainland to the Ocean City Inlet in Maryland. It separates the Atlantic from the shallow Assawoman and Little Assawoman Bays. A glance at a map shows that this strand of shore extends farther into the ocean than the rest of the Delaware coast. If you stand on the beach facing the sea, you are at the easternmost point on the Delmarva Peninsula.

This area was formerly part of Delaware Seashore State Park and is still shown as such on some maps. Read the section on beach walking in

Twilight falls over the Atlantic Ocean as waves lap a sandy beach in Fenwick Island State Park. Beyond the horizon, the next landfall is Europe.

the introduction before your trip. The trail described here begins near the town of Fenwick Island and runs north along the beach for the length of the park, returning the same way. Like any pleasant beach hike, it is ideal for maundering or dawdling; walk as much or as little as you wish.

Access

From Georgetown, drive east on US 9 for 11.9 miles to the junction with DE 1. Turn right (south) onto DE 1 and enter Fenwick Island State Park after 19.3 miles. Continue for another 2.5 miles and turn left at the entrance sign that reads FENWICK ISLAND STATE PARK BATHHOUSE. An entrance fee is charged from May 1 to October 31. Park north of the bathhouse, as close to the northern end of the parking lot as possible.

Trail

Go across the primary dune on the northernmost walkway and turn left (north) along the ocean. The beach here is set aside for swimming and surfing.

You soon enter the surf fishing area and, after almost 0.5 mile you will pass a dune crossing for off-road vehicles, followed shortly by a private inholding of beachfront condominiums. Residents will likely be crowded onto the beach during pleasant weather; make your way around the sunbathers, beach umbrellas, and blankets and continue northward.

Just beyond the condominiums you will see another off-road vehicle dune crossing, and then you walk along an isolated shore. An occasional beachcomber or fisherman, along with mixed flocks of herring, ring-billed, and great black-backed gulls, may share the solitude.

A third off-road vehicle dune crossing is encountered 2 miles from the swimming area. To complete your hike through the park, continue north another 0.5 mile to a tall, silo-like concrete tower just behind the front dune. This observation tower was one of many built along the Delaware coast during World War II to direct the fire of shore batteries against enemy ships. Most have fallen into ruin, but a few yet stand as empty columns, their narrow openings near the top still staring seaward. The houses visible on the dunes to the north, some with their porches extending over the beach, are in South Bethany. Turn and walk back to your car.

31. Eastern Shore of Virginia National Wildlife Refuge

Land's end

Hiking distance: 1.5 miles
Hiking time: 1 hour
Map: USGS Townsend; refuge map

Lying at the southern tip of the Delmarva Peninsula on Cape Charles, the Eastern Shore of Virginia National Wildlife Refuge, Delmarva's newest refuge, was created to protect a critical resting and feeding site for birds migrating along the Atlantic flyway. The U.S. Fish and Wildlife Service now owns about 1,200 acres here, and land acquisition is continuing.

Migratory birds tend to follow topographic features during their long flights. In autumn, southbound birds come down the Delmarva Peninsula by the millions, guided by the bordering bays and the seacoast. As the peninsula narrows, it becomes a great, natural funnel. When the birds reach land's end at Cape Charles, they face an arduous 19-mile flight over the open waters of the Chesapeake Bay. At the point, the weather becomes critical for land birds such as warblers, sparrows, thrushes, and hawks. If there is a strong northwest wind, crossing the open water may be deadly, since the wind could blow the birds out to sea. At such times, those that attempt the crossing may occasionally be seen beating their way back to shore, fighting the headwind with their ebbing strength. If they make it to land, they are so exhausted they can often be approached easily. Under such conditions, few birds continue their migratory flight; most stack up at Cape Charles to await better

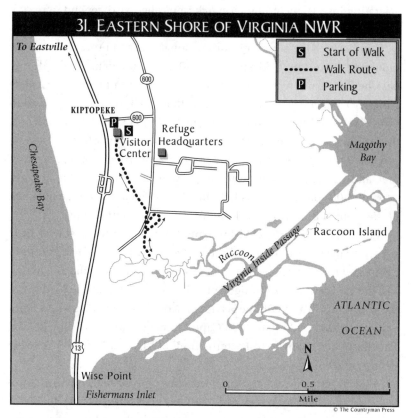

31. EASTERN SHORE OF VIRGINIA NWR

To Eastville

S Start of Walk
•••••• Walk Route
P Parking

600

KIPTOPEKE

600

Refuge Headquarters

Magothy Bay

P
S
Visitor Center

Chesapeake Bay

Raccoon Inside Passage
Virginia Inside Passage

Raccoon Island

ATLANTIC

OCEAN

13

N

Wise Point

Fishermans Inlet

0   0.5   1
Mile

© The Countryman Press

winds. When a front has brought in good weather, the birds move through the cape in great numbers and head over the Chesapeake with little hesitation.

Cape Charles is one of the most important bird migration funnels in North America, along with Cape May, New Jersey, on the north shore of Delaware Bay, and Point Pelee, Ontario, on the north shore of Lake Erie. Much remains to be learned about migrations through funnels such as Cape Charles, but it is clear the cape is used by large numbers of all sorts of birds—shorebirds, ground birds, raptors, passerines, and waterfowl. Migrating insects, including monarch butterflies, also depend upon the cape for rest and food before starting over the bay.

Numbers tell the story: millions of songbirds and more than 80,000 raptors each autumn, and as many as 100,000 monarchs *per day* during peak periods. Banding stations set up here and at nearby Kiptopeke State Park (see chapter 23) regularly net more than 800 birds annually. In addition, diverse habitats on the refuge (including salt marsh, pine forests, thickets, grasslands, freshwater and brackish ponds, and offshore islands) provide essential shelter and food for a rich assortment of winter, summer, and year-round avian residents, as well as 34 species of mammals. Close to 300 species of birds have been recorded at the refuge; it is one of the premier birding and wildlife sites on the Eastern Shore.

Man has changed the environment of the cape in the past with little regard for the birds or other wildlife. Military installations, like Fort John Curtis and the Cape Charles Air Force Station, and major thoroughfares, like the Chesapeake Bay Bridge-Tunnel, dominated land use patterns in the area. The Fish and Wildlife Service took over the Cape Charles Air Force Station in 1984 and established Cape Charles National Wildlife Refuge. The name was changed to Eastern Shore of Virginia National Wildlife Refuge in 1985.

You will see some old gun emplacements on your hike, but most military structures have been removed. The refuge is managed to create diverse habitat for wildlife. Groves of tall trees are available for forest-dependent migrating birds; low, shrubby areas are maintained for passerines; expanses of short grass are set aside for raptor hunting grounds; and scrubland and thickets are protected for ground birds such as northern bobwhite and woodcock.

Access

From the center of Eastville, drive south on US Business 13 for 1.3 miles to US 13, then continue south for another 14 miles to VA 600 in the hamlet of Kiptopeke. Turn left and drive 0.1 mile to the visitor center on the right.

The butterfly garden near the Eastern Shore of Virginia National Wildlife Refuge Visitor Center attracts flower-loving resident and migratory insects. The building has been hailed as one of the finest visitor centers in the national wildlife refuge system.

Trail

Your easy walk begins on the Butterfly Trail at the visitor center. Take time to tour the visitor center before you hike. Informational leaflets, species lists, and maps are available, along with exhibits and programs. There is a wildlife viewing area and a butterfly garden. The center is open January and February on Friday to Sunday from 10 to 2, March daily from 10 to 2, April through November daily from 9 to 4, and December daily from 10 to 2. You can begin the Butterfly Trail out the back door, or if the center is closed, pick up your trail to the right of the building at the right end of the parking lot.

The 0.5-mile Butterfly Trail is a wide, mowed swath through shrubby old fields. Goldenrods, pokeweed, groundsel tree, black locust, and wax myrtle are common plants along the way. Insects are plentiful, including butterflies, dragonflies, gnats, grasshoppers, crickets, beetles, and many,

many others. The trail ends at a parking area, where there is an information kiosk. You will return to this spot later, but continue your hike by turning right on the broad, 0.5-mile Wildlife Trail that begins on the right side of the parking lot.

The way curves left on a gravel path and very shortly reaches the first of two short spur trails. On the left, steep steps rise to an observation overlook on top of the World War II–era Winslow Bunker. The 16-inch gun emplacement, now empty and covered with dense brush and saplings, is a great place for bird watching. The climb rewards you with an unmatched view of the refuge and surrounding countryside. Small birds flit about the shrubs and trees at eye level. Hawks and vultures soar by just above your head. You may also see small boats sailing along the Virginia Inside Passage out in the marsh. The passage is a dredged channel that provides a protected shortcut for craft traveling between the Chesapeake and Magothy Bays. On the far eastern horizon the shimmering breakers of the open ocean can be seen on a clear day.

After descending, turn left and walk a few steps to a T-junction. The second spur leads right and soon comes upon the small, Fitchett-Hallett family cemetery on the right. Tombstones tell of burials stretching over more than a century, with the oldest markers dating from the early 1800s.

The way continues to an overlook deck set on a low, wooded bluff overlooking an expansive salt marsh. The platform is a good vantage point for sighting waterfowl or wading birds and for tracing the intricacies of Raccoon Creek and its tributaries that thread the tidal marsh. Birdlife is abundant; on my last visit, I stepped onto the deck and immediately spotted osprey, merlin, northern harrier, belted kingfisher, common yellowthroat, and several other species that disappeared from view before I could identify them. The Smith Island Lighthouse is visible on the Atlantic shore, about 3 miles away.

Walk back by the graveyard to the main trail, but this time continue straight, keeping the Winslow Bunker on your left. These are among the best ruins of fortifications in Virginia. They not only have historical value but also serve as bat roosting areas; nine species of bats make their home in the refuge. The trail passes through a maritime forest of loblolly pine and American holly and then turns left to tunnel under one of the gun emplacements.

On the other side, the path curves left through a thicket and arrives back at the information kiosk near the parking lot. Follow the Butterfly Trail back to the visitor center and your waiting car.

32. Chincoteague National Wildlife Refuge

A day hike on Assateague Island

Hiking distance: 8.5 miles
Hiking time: 4.5 hours
Maps: USGS Chincoteague East; refuge map

Assateague is a textbook example of a barrier island, a physiographic feature occurring regularly along the American coast from Massachusetts to Texas. Although common to the Atlantic and Gulf Coasts of the United States, barrier islands are found only along less than 10 percent of all the earth's shorelines. Assateague Island lies just off the mainland of Maryland and Virginia. It is a long, narrow ribbon of sand, stretching 37 miles in a north-south direction, but is only between 0.2 and 3 miles wide.

Islands like Assateague are believed to have been formed at the end of or sometime after the last great ice age—perhaps 6,000 to 10,000 years ago. This part of North America was not glaciated, but the area felt the influence of the ice far to the north. As the continental glaciers melted, ocean waters rose, and mighty inland rivers carried great loads of sediment that were deposited along the coast. The result was the development of a broad continental shelf with shallow waters offshore. Over the millennia, winds and tides combined with ocean waves to redistribute the old river sediments and to create narrow islands of fine sand.

Although thousands of years old, Assateague is, geologically speaking, an infant. It can be described as being storm built, for it is during

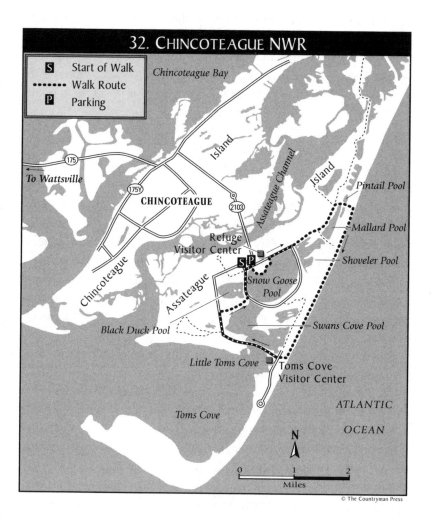

severe ocean storms that the great sculpting forces do most of their work. Most landscape features such as dunes on Assateague are probably the result of forces that occurred within a human lifespan. Even these features can be very short-lived, since high winds and tides can change the appearance of the island in just a day or two.

Born of the sea and continually shaped by it, the island seems more related to the world of water than to that of land. It is an essential part of that "ultimate wilderness that will never be tamed by men," as Jonathon Norton Leonard called the ocean. Protection for the wild character of Assateague seems assured because the entire island is preserved as public land. The Virginia portion was set aside as Chincoteague National Wildlife Refuge in 1943. A few small islands in the Maryland waters of Chincoteague Bay are also part of the refuge.

The island can be reached via bridges from the mainland. This easy access, as well as the rewarding spectacle of animals (including Assateague's famous wild ponies), makes Chincoteague one of the most visited national wildlife refuges in the country. Visitation reaches its highest levels on summer weekends, when there may be more cars attempting to cross over to the island than there are parking spaces available.

This day hike follows boardwalks, trails, paved and unpaved roads, and the Atlantic shore to explore many of the island's wildlife habitats: marshland, pools, forests, dunes, and beach. Read the recommendations on beach walking in the introduction before starting.

About 0.8 mile of your walk is on the Wildlife Loop, a 3.2-mile paved road through some of the most rewarding sections of the refuge. The circuit is closed to cars until 3 PM each day so that hikers and bicyclists can enjoy the wildlife and scenery, but note that the loop opens to vehicles at 9 AM for nine days in November during the refuge's observance of Waterfowl Week from the Saturday before Thanksgiving to the Sunday following the holiday. In addition, about 1 mile of your hike is on an unpaved service road that is open to hikers and also used by official vehicles, including an air-conditioned tour bus operated by the Chincoteague Natural History Association. The bus tours are conducted three times a day every day from June to September, once or twice a day on Friday, Saturday, and Sunday in April and May, and once a day on weekends in March, October, and most of November. Reservations are required and a fee is charged. The service road is also open to public vehicular traffic from noon to 3:30 for four days (from Thanksgiving to the Sunday fol-

A herd of wild horses grazes on wash flats in Chincoteague National Wildlife Refuge. They are believed to be descended from domestic horses released on Assateague Island by 17th-century colonial farmers.

lowing the holiday) during Waterfowl Week each November. The service road is closed to hikers during hunting season, usually in December and part of January, except on Wednesday, Saturday, and Sunday, when there is no hunting. Call the refuge at 757-336-6122 if you have questions. The Chincoteague Natural History Association can be reached at 757-336-3696.

Mosquitoes and other biting insects on the island hungrily attack anything that offers a blood meal. You may gain an appreciation of the voraciousness of the mosquitoes if you realize that operators of the Chincoteague Natural History Association bus do not open the windows or doors during their two-hour tour of the refuge. Insect repellent is an absolute necessity for hikers during the warmer months.

Horses wander about the island at will. Observe them from a distance; they are wild and can inflict severe injuries by biting and kicking. Dogs are not permitted on Chincoteague National Wildlife Refuge.

A backpacking trek on Assateague Island in both Maryland and Virginia is described in chapter 33, where you will also find more information on the island and its history.

Access

From Accomac, drive north on US Business 13 for 2 miles. Continue north on US 13 for 2.5 miles, and then turn right (north) onto VA 679, a country road that makes unexpected, unmarked twists and bends. In 10.2 miles (about 5.4 miles north of Modest Town), fork left. At a minor crossroads 1 mile north of Atlantic (13.6 miles from US 13), turn left. Go another 1.4 miles to Wattsville and turn right (east) onto VA 175. Drive 7.8 miles to the town of Chincoteague on Chincoteague Island. Turn left (north) onto VA 175Y (Main Street). In 0.4 mile, turn right onto VA 2103 (Maddox Boulevard). This road crosses the Assateague Channel and enters Chincoteague National Wildlife Refuge after 1.7 miles. An entrance fee is charged. Just 0.5 mile farther, turn left into the Chincoteague Refuge Visitor Center parking area. For this hike, park at the far side of the lot near the Freshwater Marsh Trail entrance (marked by a sign). The visitor center provides information, exhibits, maps, pamphlets, drinking water, and restrooms. It is open daily from 9 to 5 during the summer and from 9 to 4 during the rest of the year.

Trail

The 1-mile Freshwater Marsh Trail begins on a boardwalk through loblolly pines. You very shortly reach the Wildlife Loop where the boardwalk ends. You will return to this spot later, but for now cross the pavement and continue straight on the Freshwater Marsh Trail. Numbered stations along the way are keyed to a descriptive pamphlet. If you forgot to pick up a pamphlet at the visitor center, they are also available here from a box.

The trail follows a semicircular dike separating an impounded wetlands on the left from Snow Goose Pond on the right. After about 0.5 mile you reach an observation platform. Take advantage of the overlook to see the marsh and Snow Goose Pond from a higher perspective—an infrequent opportunity in this horizontal expanse of marsh and sky. Mounted binoculars and a telescope provided at the platform enable you to get views of distant waterfowl or long-legged wading birds.

The trail bends back to the Wildlife Loop. Turn right. After about 0.3 mile, continue straight on an unpaved service road where the paved Wildlife Loop curves to the right. Step around the gate to gain access to the service road.

The service road begins in a loblolly pine forest, but the trees soon thin on the right, affording views of Shoveler Pool. This pond is one of 11 such impoundments on the refuge, maintained to provide favored habitat and food plants for migrating waterfowl. The pools collect fresh water from rains but also can be inundated with salt water. Their depth and salinity are closely regulated, and some pools are lowered periodically. From October to March, the pools and marshes will likely be crowded with many species of ducks and geese, especially snow geese. These glistening white birds with black wing tips are perhaps partially responsible for establishing the refuge. Dwindling numbers of snow geese and other waterfowl alerted biologists in the early 1900s to the necessity of providing feeding and resting areas for birds in the coastal marshes along their migratory routes.

After about 0.5 mile, you reach a side lane (closed to entry) on the right that leads along C Dike separating Shoveler Pool and Mallard Pool. Mallard Pool has very little open water; it is mostly marshland with dense stands of emergent vegetation. Views across the marsh reach all the way to the dunes facing the Atlantic. The area on the left of the service road is upland forest dominated by loblolly pine.

Continue straight past the side lane for about another 0.5 mile and reach an intersection—the first cross trail you encounter since leaving the Wildlife Loop. The way to the left is posted as Area 5 and is closed to the public. The lane going right is marked with a wooden post with the letter *D* for D Dike. Turn right and walk along D Dike, which separates Mallard Pool from Pintail Pool. This stretch of the hike can be one of the best places to see shorebirds. Willet, greater yellowlegs, and dunlin are some of the species that feed on the mudflats.

D Dike extends to the back dunes. Use the dune crossing walkway and come out onto the ocean beach. Turn right and walk south. The oceanfront is a major attraction for refuge visitors in the summer, but with about 10 miles of wild beach it is likely that you will enjoy long stretches of solitude, even on summer weekends and holidays. Your walk covers more than 3.25 miles of beachfront.

Reach the Toms Cove area of the island, marked by utility poles visible behind the front dune. Turn right, cross through the dunes, and walk through the parking lot to paved Beach Road. Toms Cove Visitor Center, on the left, has drinking water and restrooms.

Follow Beach Road across the causeway that separates Little Toms Cove on the left from Swans Cove Pool on the right. The walk along the road rewards you with excellent views of marshland and additional chances to see birds and other wildlife. After about 1.25 miles, the paved Black Duck Trail begins on the right side of Beach Road at an intersection where a road leads left to the Woodland Trail trailhead.

Follow the 1-mile Black Duck Trail as it parallels the road on the left and a ditch on the right. The marshy ditch is a good place to watch great blue herons stalking the shallows for prey or to see big turtles basking on the banks or logs.

The Black Duck Trail makes a 90-degree turn to the right and leads through a forest of loblolly pine, sassafras, and sweet gum, with a diverse shrub layer of dwarf sumac, bayberry, and other woody plants. The forest gives way to open marsh on both sides of the trail, with Black Duck Pool on the left and Swans Cove Pool on the right. Appropriately, American black ducks are often seen along this stretch of the Black Duck Trail.

The trail ends at the Wildlife Loop. Snow Goose Pond is visible ahead and the Assateague Island Lighthouse looms above the trees to your left. Turn left and follow the road for 0.5 mile to the Freshwater Marsh Trail. Go left on the boardwalk to return to the visitor center parking lot.

33. Assateague Island

Walking by the sea

Hiking distance: 25 miles
Hiking time: three days, two nights
Maps: USGS Tingles Island, Whittington Point, Boxiron, and
    Chincoteague East; national seashore map

A ssateague is the richest and liveliest of the Atlantic barrier islands. Created and dominated by the sea, the island is home to wild horses, to
harmless reptiles like the terrestrial hognose snake and the marine logger-
head turtle, and to aggressive (some say offensive) arthropods like ticks, salt
marsh mosquitoes, and biting flies such as greenheads, deerflies, sand flies,
and stable flies. Birds live here too—more than three hundred species have
been recorded. They include soaring vultures, ten different kinds of hawks
(including the rarely seen peregrine falcon), bald eagle, and four species of
owls. A wide array of thousands of wading birds, shorebirds, and waterfowl can be seen on Assateague. The American oystercatcher, the only bird
of its kind in the eastern United States, uses its heavy, orange beak to pry
between the hard shells of bivalves and to dine on the meat within. Loons,
those symbols of wildness and far-off places, dive for fish in the winter
surf. Little birds like marsh wren are more often heard than seen among the
tall reeds and grasses. Yellow-rumped warbler, unlike its insect-eating
cousins, is found here even in winter because it feeds on the clusters of light
gray fruit from the northern bayberry. You can also find seaside sparrow,
swallows, bobolink, droves of red-winged blackbird, and even tree-loving
species like the brown-headed nuthatch, which nests in the thick pine and
oak forests near the southern end of the island.

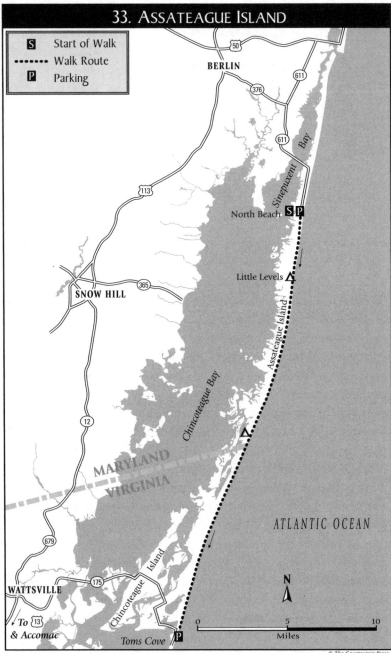

33. ASSATEAGUE ISLAND

S	Start of Walk
••••••	Walk Route
P	Parking

BERLIN

North Beach

Little Levels

SNOW HILL

Chincoteague Bay

Sinepuxent Bay

Assateague Island

MARYLAND

VIRGINIA

ATLANTIC OCEAN

WATTSVILLE

To 13
& Accomac

Chincoteague Island

Toms Cove

N

0		5		10

Miles

© The Countryman Press

There is also a nice variety of mammals on Assateague. In addition to horses (by far the island's best known inhabitants), there are red fox, raccoon, white-tailed deer, sika (Japanese elk), opossum, muskrat, river otter, eastern cottontail, and the endangered Delmarva fox squirrel. At least seven different species of marine mammals occur in the ocean, often seen swimming offshore and sometimes found beached and dying on the sands.

The sea casts up an amazing variety of creatures and their remains upon the strand: an array of shells, starfish, crabs, Atlantic horseshoe crab, sponges, jellyfish, sand dollars, shark teeth, whelk egg cases, fish— the list is almost endless. Assateague is blessed with many animals, some unusual, some unpleasant, but all—in their way—beautiful.

The island is one of the last along the Atlantic where the visitor can see a bit of nature in its pure state. All of Assateague is preserved as public land: Assateague Island National Seashore (managed by the National Park Service), Chincoteague National Wildlife Refuge (managed by the U.S. Fish and Wildlife Service), and Assateague State Park (managed by the Maryland Park Service). Here, thick stands of beach grass create sand dunes and a place for other plants to gain a foothold. The hardy seaside goldenrod colors the dunes with its bright flower plumes from August to December. Seabeach evening primrose inches along the sand, its silvery white leaves covered with fine hairs that help retard evaporation of the plant's internal water supply. It has large, bright-yellow blossoms that open in the late afternoon and close in the early morning.

The light seems a little more striking here than anywhere else on Delmarva—the sunrises, sunsets, the moon and stars a little more brilliant—and the air is almost always pure and clean. Cradling the island on all sides are the changing but eternal tides. After a few days on Assateague, you become attuned to the motion of the planet and the universe. The celestial drama in the wide sky combines with the steady roar of the waves and the ceaseless wind to fill the air with the constancy of the elements in action.

Assateague is brushed by centuries of superstition, legend, and history, recently marked with heavy-handed attempts by man to forge a permanent presence. Still, the island remains a bastion of wildness, relatively undisturbed by the encroachments of civilization. We have few such places remaining in our ravaged, overcrowded world. Not many areas are better than the fastness of Assateague for a long walk under the sun, through the wind, by the sea.

This chapter describes a 25-mile backpacking trek on Assateague Island, beginning at North Beach, Maryland, and going south to Toms Cove, Virginia. The walk is divided into three days and two nights, with daily hiking distances of 4, 8.5, and 12.5 miles.

The hike can be shortened if you lack the time or the inclination for a long trip. If you just want to sample a bit of the Assateague backcountry, consider turning the first day's trek—4 miles from North Beach to Little Levels—into an 8-mile-long day hike. The island also offers other opportunities for shorter walks. See chapter 32 for an 8.5-mile hike in the Virginia portion of Assateague, with comments on the island's formation and geology. Day hikers will also enjoy beach walking along the island's isolated north shore (you can walk all the way to the Ocean City Inlet) and to the island's southern end at Fishing Point on curving Toms Cove Hook. Short walks can be taken on the national seashore's three nature trails in Maryland and on the national wildlife refuge's five trails in Virginia. Maps and other trail information are available at the visitor centers.

Barrier island backpacking is an invigorating challenge. You walk along the ocean beach or (in Maryland) on a sandy track called the Back Trail, which is behind the primary dune. Careful planning and preparation are necessary for an enjoyable, trouble-free trek. First, read the section on beach walking in the introduction. Since you will be out for three days, more attention must be given to specific details. The National Park Service issues a leaflet with recommendations and regulations for backcountry travel.

This hike is not for the novice. I have seen even experienced backpackers falter and fail along the way. The insects, wind, and sun can combine to demoralize the unprepared hiker. Added to these discomforts is the physical effort of walking for miles through deep sand, especially when carrying a heavy pack. "Hiking five miles on Assateague is as strenuous as hiking ten or twelve miles in the mountains," a park ranger told me. Blisters, even on trail-hardened feet, are a common occurrence, so come equipped with adequate first-aid supplies.

The blazing sun is the first consideration; you cannot escape it. Sunburn or, worse, heatstroke and dehydration are backcountry emergencies that can be avoided by a sunscreen cream and adequate supplies of water. Sunglasses and a hat are added precautions to be included in your gear. No potable water is available in the backcountry; you must carry all water with you. The National Park Service recommends a minimum of 1 gallon per person per day (that amounts to about 25 pounds of water per person for this three-day trek). A friend and I carried slightly less than 1 gallon per person per day on this hike (in relatively cool weather in April); we had very little left at the end. Some Assateague backpackers carry canned foods instead of freeze-dried foods that require water for cooking.

The wind is constant and sometimes very strong. It blows sand into your boots, tent, stove, and food. Tent pegs work loose under the tugging of the gusts. To prevent a tent from collapsing on top of you in the middle of the night, use special pegs designed to anchor in soft sand. I make my own pegs out of quarter-inch wooden dowels, cut 15 inches long and notched to hold the guy ropes. I drive the entire peg into the sand and use a small, plastic trowel to dig it out when breaking camp. Pack a couple of extra pegs in case they break or get lost in the sand drifts. Even hot, summer days can turn into cool, breezy nights, so a windbreaker is a necessary addition.

Backpackers must be armored against the legions of bloodsucking insects inhabiting the island. The voracious feeding of salt marsh mosquitoes must be experienced to be appreciated. They are usually discouraged by repellents, but I discovered that heavy rains wash off repellent while not thwarting the mosquitoes at all. Staying on the beach is another fairly successful way to avoid most of the mosquitoes, because they are deterred by the strong winds. The wild ponies have learned this trick and often spend their time on the beach. High winds generally do not stop the strong-flying greenheads. These are big insects that bite painfully; most repellents seem ineffective against them. Greenhead season on the island leads you to appreciate the night, since these insects fly and feed only during the day.

Because of the biting insects, some backpackers plan their trips for early spring or late fall when insects are not on the wing. Indeed, the time of year should be a major consideration as you plan your hike. Warm summer weekends and holidays bring the most visitors to the island. Despite the crowds, however, the backcountry is often mostly deserted. After June and well into September, the ocean is warm enough for swimming. Prior to May and after the first killing frost in autumn, insects are not a nuisance, the weather is often mild, and there are fewer people. Winter backpacking along the ocean can be severe and requires special knowledge and equipment. Whatever the season, be prepared for sudden and dramatic shifts in weather. I recall a hike along the shore in August when the skies became overcast and a howling onshore wind drove salt spray up the beach all the way to the front dune. The moisture and wind combined to create very chilly conditions that could have led to hypothermia in unwary hikers. Hypothermia—a severe lowering of the body core temperature—is a life-threatening condition that can happen at any time of the year. Fatigue, wind, and wet clothing worsen the threat. During extremely adverse weather, such as hurricanes and northeasters, the hike should not be attempted. Adequate warning of these major storms is usually provided by forecasts. Locally severe thunderstorms with lightning pose special problems, since you are the highest object on the beach. Seek shelter among the dunes and wait out the storm.

One of the lingering memories of your trip will be the fragrance of burning driftwood in your campfire or cooking fire. However, adequate supplies of driftwood for cooking are by no means assured, so you need to carry a small, lightweight stove with enough fuel for three days. A windscreen and hurricane matches that do not snuff out in the wind should be included.

Backcountry travel on the island is managed by the National Park Service. They maintain two backcountry campsites for the exclusive use of overnight hikers. The sites are near the ocean, behind the primary dune. Four additional areas set up for canoe or kayak camping can also be used by backpackers; all these latter campsites are on the bay side. All six areas are in Maryland. Each site is equipped with a picnic table and a chemical toilet. This trek uses the two hike-in campsites, but other hikes can be planned using the paddle-in sites. Small signs along the beach and along the Back Trail plainly point the way to the campsites. Always be aware of your location, because the signs may have been destroyed during storms. Camping elsewhere in the backcountry is prohibited.

The two hike-in areas along the ocean side are usually open year-round, but one or both of the sites may be closed in the spring and summer because of shorebird nesting. The species of concern is piping plover. From mid-March through August this threatened bird nests on stretches of high beach or inner dunes where bits of shells or pebbles are present. Any disturbance or intrusion into the plover's nesting territory forces the parents to leave the nest, thus seriously jeopardizing the survival of the eggs or young chicks. Each year the National Park Service locates nesting sites and marks them with fences and warning signs. Whether or not warning signs are posted, hikers are advised to watch for any nesting activity and give wide berth.

The four paddle-in sites on the bay side are closed for about three weeks during hunting season, usually during the second half of October and again in late November and early December. The National Park Service discourages camping on the bay side during the summer because of the high numbers of ravenous insects.

Kilometer markers (KM) are placed on the ocean side of the front dune along the route in Maryland. After leaving North Beach, KM 16 is the first post you will encounter. KM 35 is the last post, just north of the Maryland-Virginia border. Two emergency telephones are located along the Back Trail near KM 21.5 and at the dune crossing near KM 29.1.

They can be used by hikers, paddlers, hunters, and anglers during emergencies to request assistance. Dogs are not allowed on this hike.

Part of the island traversed by the walk in Maryland is also used by off-road vehicles (ORVs). Be alert for vehicles approaching from behind while walking on the beach. Sometimes the sound of the surf drowns out engine noise. ORVs are not allowed on the Back Trail.

Backcountry permits must be obtained in person before you start your trip; no reservations are accepted, and a fee is charged. Permits can be picked up at either the Toms Cove Visitor Center or the North Beach Ranger Station, but it is better to obtain them at the latter place for this hike. The National Park Service strictly adheres to designated check-in times to allow sufficient daylight for you to reach your campsite. For this trek, permits have to be picked up at the North Beach Ranger Station no later than two hours before sunset. Also note that once your permit is issued, you cannot change your itinerary. For current information on permits, campsite closures, fees, sunset times, or other details, contact Assateague Island National Seashore, 7206 National Seashore Lane, Berlin, MD 21811 (telephone 410-641-3030 or 757-336-6577). The Web site is www.nps.gov/asis.

Access

This hike requires two vehicles. To drop off the first car, drive south from Snow Hill on MD 12 for 12.2 miles to the Virginia line. There the highway becomes VA 679. Continue south for another 7.6 miles to Wattsville and VA 175. Turn left (east) and go 7.8 miles to the town of Chincoteague on Chincoteague Island. Turn left (north) onto VA 175Y (Main Street). In 0.4 mile, turn right onto VA 2113 (Maddox Boulevard). This road goes straight across Assateague Channel, entering Assateague Island National Seashore and Chincoteague National Wildlife Refuge after 1.7 miles. An entrance fee, valid for seven days, is charged for each vehicle. Continue driving down this road (here known as Beach Road) for 3 miles to Toms Cove Visitor Center. Check in at the visitor center to get directions on where to park overnight.

If coming from Accomac, go north on US Business 13 for 2 miles, and then continue north on US 13 for 2.5 miles to VA 679. Turn right (north) and be alert, because this country road makes unmarked turns. In 10.2 miles (about 5.4 miles north of Modest Town), keep left at a fork. At a minor crossroads 1 mile north of Atlantic (13.6 miles from US 13), turn left. Drive another 1.4 miles to Wattsville and turn right onto VA 175. Follow the above directions to Assateague Island.

Having parked a car at the Toms Cove Visitor Center, drive the other vehicle back to Wattsville and turn right (north) on VA 679. Enter Maryland and continue north on MD 12 for 10.5 miles to US 113. Turn right (north). Drive 15.6 miles to MD 376 in Berlin and turn right (east). This highway ends at MD 611 after 4 miles; turn right (south). You will pass the Barrier Island Visitor Center on the right after 3 miles. Just beyond, cross Sinepuxent Bay on the Verrazzano Bridge (named for the first white explorer in these waters) and arrive on Assateague. When on the island, turn right at the first opportunity onto Bayberry Drive. (The road that leads straight enters Assateague State Park.) The vehicle fee you paid earlier in Virginia is valid for entry. After reaching the seashore, turn left into the North Beach parking lot. Stop at the ranger station to obtain your backcountry permit. Remember that permits must be issued no later than two hours before sunset to allow enough time for you to walk to your first night's campsite. Parking spaces near the ranger station are reserved for backpackers.

DAY 1

North Beach to Little Levels
Hiking distance: 4 miles
Hiking time: 2.5 hours

Follow one of the walkways across the dunes and turn right (south) along the ocean. North Beach is a major recreation area for seashore visitors, featuring camping, picnicking, and swimming. Around the turn of the

Stunted trees and windswept grasses mantle a back dune on Assateague Island.

20th century there was a small settlement here. The community of North Beach consisted only of a few houses, a one-room school, a saltworks, and a lifesaving station. The station was staffed by hardy men of the U.S. Life Saving Service, a forerunner of the Coast Guard. Equipped and trained to rescue shipwrecked mariners and to assist in salvaging stranded vessels, the surfmen, as they were called, risked their lives in the pounding gales and battering surf. The North Beach station was operational from 1884 to 1954, first under the Life Saving Service and later under the Coast Guard.

On our walk, we had hiked only a short distance when we saw our first wild horses—two of them, standing near the top of the front dune. They turned and wandered away slowly as we drew near. Do not attempt to approach the horses too closely. They bite and kick and can inflict serious injuries.

Assateague's ponies are said to have descended from Spanish horses that swam ashore from ancient galleons cracked up in ocean storms, but the tales are legend, with no proof and little credibility. It has also been claimed that the wild ponies of Assateague are descendants of horses left behind by pirates, but again there is no source material for verification.

Hard evidence gathered by historians shows that the barrier islands off the Maryland and Virginia coasts were used by colonists in the 17th century for grazing horses, cattle, and sheep. The outlying marshes and beaches were remote and not easily accessible. As a result, they were not settled and belonged to the county government. Mainland farmers leased the outer lands and used them as a sort of pasture commons or open range. Domestic animals were ferried from the bay-side farms by barge or scow or sometimes driven across narrow stretches of water at low tide.

By the late 1600s, the American wilderness was already disappearing under the assault of more people, more cropland, and more regulations. Horses had become such a nuisance in colonial Virginia that the Assembly enacted a law in 1669 forbidding the importation of new horses, imposing a tax on all resident horses, and requesting that owners keep their horses in pens between July 20 and October 20. In 1691 new laws enabled planters, under certain circumstances, to kill horses found trespassing and causing depredations. Open grazing on remote islands was a way for colonial farmers to avoid the expensive requirement that livestock be fenced to avoid damage to crops. Horses and other animals permitted to roam on the islands were generally branded by their owners for identification.

Today's horses on Assateague are descended from the stock placed there by colonial farmers. The feral ponies are believed to have reached their present size (smaller than a standard horse and larger than a Shetland pony) as a result of generations of inbreeding, subsisting on the coarse salt marsh grass, and perhaps continual exposure to the harsh elements of Assateague.

Beyond the South Beach swimming area, ORVs use the beach. If you are here during a time when the hungry insects are not abundant, you may want to walk along the Back Trail. The old road behind the front dune was used to reach vacation cottages and lodges when the island was still in private ownership. Part of this track was known as Baltimore

Avenue in the 1950s, when Ocean Beach Corporation owned most of the Maryland portion of the island. Other developers had been at work on Assateague, but Ocean Beach brought sophisticated techniques and massive capital to develop the island systematically by dividing the land into small-lot offerings. The company mounted an aggressive sales campaign that included large-scale advertising, colorful promotion, and personal contacts by representatives. By 1962, the company had sold 5,850 lots, had paved Baltimore Avenue, bulldozed side roads, and installed electric lines. They were moving toward establishment of hotels and shopping centers and building a bridge to the mainland.

In March of that year, a severe northeaster struck the island, completely demolishing most of the houses that had been built. It was the area's most destructive storm of the 20th century, exceeding in fury even the hurricanes that sometimes batter the coast. The North Atlantic, driven ashore by high winds and tides, surged across the island all the way to the bay at several points. The electrical lines snapped, and Baltimore Avenue and other roads were washed away in most places. Remnants of broken and crumbling asphalt can still be found along the Back Trail or scattered among the dunes. It is now a road to nowhere, waiting to completely disappear with the next storm or to be buried under sand.

After the water subsided and the immensity of the loss was assessed, Ocean Beach and other private interests petitioned the federal government to engineer protection for the island from natural forces. Studies showed that the cost would be prohibitive, so the requests for federal assistance were denied. The great storm stilled private land speculation long enough to permit establishment of Assateague Island National Seashore in 1965.

Little Levels, your campsite for the night, is 4 miles from North Beach. It lies at a fairly wide part of the island, with extensive wash flats occurring bayward of the camp. On our trip, the sun was nearing the horizon as we scoured the flats for firewood. A red fox loped across the barren expanse, starting on its nightly hunt, and in the far distance a stallion drove his small herd of mares and foals over the brow of the dune onto the beach.

DAY 2

Little Levels to State Line
Hiking distance: 8.5 miles
Hiking time: 5 hours

You will almost certainly encounter surf fishermen on the Maryland portion of Assateague at all times of the year. They drive into the backcountry in their ORVs and cast baited lines into the ocean in quest of black drum, striped bass, flounder, white perch, bluefish, and many others.

In the autumn you may also see hunters (mainly on the bay side) because Assateague Island is one of the few national parks that allow hunting and trapping. Congress specifically included hunting as a recreational use of the seashore when it was established. Sportsmen rush to the island during legal seasons, going after sika, white-tailed deer, mourning dove, Canada goose, snow goose, brant, scaups, scoters, eiders, long-tailed duck, mallard, American black duck, wood duck, mergansers, mottled duck, blue-winged teal, green-winged teal, common pintail, gadwall, northern shoveler, and other animals.

State Line, your second campsite of the trek, is nestled among the dunes about 1 mile north of the Maryland-Virginia border. Nighttime at State Line can be immense, grand, and mysterious under a starlit sky. The island evokes a sense of isolation far removed in distance and time from mainland activity. At dusk, the rotating beacon of the Assateague Island light (more than 11 miles away) comes into view, sweeping across the heavens in a soft, diffuse arc. The lighthouse, built in 1867, is near the southern end of the island; its 800,000-candlepower-rated light can be seen for 19 nautical miles, warning ships of the treacherous shoals that lie just offshore.

At certain times at night on the beach during warm weather, you may be surprised to see light from an entirely different source. Waves crashing onto the shore flash with an eerie, greenish glimmer just as the top breaks into foam. Sometimes the entire face of a long breaker will light up in sequence, resembling a dancing chain reaction down the beach. The strange, fiery light is caused by billions of tiny phosphorescent protozoa, part of the rich pelagic life of the North Atlantic. Countless numbers of these microorganisms are cast onto the beach with every wave. When you walk across wet sand at low tide, the protozoa luminesce in sparkling, radiating, star-shaped bursts of cold light. Tracing patterns in the sand with your fingers has the same result; I felt like a wizard with magic beams of light at my fingertips. These minute creatures evidently shine when they are excited by being tossed by waves, jarred by a footfall, joggled by a finger, or perhaps stimulated by their neighbors. The protozoa glow softly and ghostlike for a few moments as they cling to your wet, sandy skin.

The beach at night is alive with many other animals. Small phosphorescent shrimp can also be found along the swash marks. Farther up the beach, on drier sand, your flashlight beam will likely intercept ghost crabs. Living in damp burrows in the sand by day, these small crabs emerge in great numbers at night to scavenge the beach and to soak in the surf. Although essentially terrestrial, they retain a close link to the sea, returning by necessity to the water to wet their gills and to lay eggs. Young ghost crabs reveal their marine ancestry by becoming part of the open ocean plankton. Although ghost crabs will remain momentarily immobilized by your flashlight beam, they soon dart away so quickly it is impossible to track them. Their protective coloration and lightning swiftness enable them to seemingly vanish.

DAY 3

State Line to Toms Cove
Hiking distance: 12.5 miles
Hiking time: 8 hours

Assateague has saved its best and most dramatic beach for the last day. Your hike continues south for about 1 mile and enters Chincoteague National Wildlife Refuge. This maritime wilderness in Virginia brings to mind the words of Henry David Thoreau, who, walking the beach on Cape Cod in another century, wrote, "The solitude was that of the ocean and desert combined."

A fence bisects the island at the border. It keeps the pony herds of the two states separate (the Virginia horses are owned by the Chincoteague Volunteer Fire Department) and also prevents ORVs from crossing into Virginia. No vehicles are permitted for the next 11.5 miles.

The wild, lonely shore is a beachcomber's paradise. We could not resist adding slightly to the weight of our packs by collecting many of the shells we came across. Shells recently washed ashore were near the surf, still gleaming with moisture, while high on the beach a long windrow of flotsam yielded other relics. In just a short distance, we found scallops, coquinas, slipper and jingle shells, and many others. Successful shell collecting is dependent upon the slope and shape of the beach, ocean currents, presence or absence of offshore sandbars, and proper timing. The best time for finding shells and other remains cast ashore is when the tide is out. Extra low tides occur immediately after a new or full moon.

About a mile north of Toms Cove and the end of our hike, we saw two Atlantic horseshoe crabs swimming ashore. Since it was spring, with night coming on, they were almost certainly washing in on a high tide to lay and fertilize eggs. The smaller male was clinging to the back of the much larger female. He would hold on to her as she crawled to just below the average high-water mark. There she would hollow out small depressions in the sand and lay eggs; he would then deposit sperm on top of them.

A particularly rough breaker caught the two, breaking the male's hold, and sent them both tumbling up the beach. The male was lucky enough to catch the retreating wave and ride it back into the sea, quickly disappearing under the dark water. The gravid female was thrown higher and landed upside down, her 10 legs splaying skyward and grasping only air. Now, if unable to right herself, she was in danger either of being stranded by the tide and left to dry out or of being eaten by gulls at dawn.

I scooped up the 2-foot-long female by resting her hard, dorsal shell in the palm of my hand. As a big wave surged landward, I gave a long heave, sending her out as far as I could. She landed upside down with a big splash, righted herself in the water, and dropped out of sight. An increasing wind from an approaching storm was blowing offshore, and that breeze, combined with a local current, might increase her prospects of finding another mate and laying her eggs.

Horseshoe crabs are remarkably adapted to the timeless rhythms of the ocean, having existed almost unchanged for more than 350 million years. They likely came out of the ancient seas to lay their eggs on land to escape now-extinct marine predators, eons before birds appeared on earth. Over untold millennia, birds evolved and began to take advantage of the crab resource. In the present age, gulls and other scavengers pick at stranded carcasses, and migratory shorebirds feast on the tiny eggs. The primitive horseshoe crabs outlived their seagoing predators and withstand the modern feathered onslaught from the skies. Now they face new threats.

Horseshoe crabs are inedible to humans, but, like birds, we have learned to take advantage of the resource. Commercial fishermen capture them for bait to harvest eels and whelks (also known as conches). Hauled from coastal waters in record numbers since 1991, horseshoe crabs satisfy the demand for jellied eel in Germany, *scungili* in Italy, or conch Creole in the Dominican Republic. Since horseshoe crabs have a life expectancy of more than 20 years and a female cannot lay eggs until she reaches 9 or 10, the negative impacts of accelerated harvesting rates that started in the early 1990s are now being seen in nature.

Horseshoe crabs are also collected in lesser numbers for biomedical research. Substances found in their blood are used to diagnose some bacterial infections in humans and to make pharmaceuticals. Throw in ocean pollution and habitat loss due to beachfront development on top of medical needs and bait harvesting, and the result is that horseshoe crabs are not nearly as plentiful as in the past.

It now seems important to save individuals like the big female. Her new opportunity, and the twenty thousand or so eggs she may lay each spring, might help horseshoe crabs weather these latest changes in their long history. Of greater help may be the annual quotas that have been imposed by the federal government and some coastal states on the number of horseshoe crabs that can be taken.

I hope the populations rebound. I hope future spring walks along the shore are still filled with clattering horseshoe crabs reenacting their age-old rituals, as they have for hundreds of millions of previous springs. To see primordial horseshoe crabs is to have a direct experience with the immense flow of time and the endless cycles of the earth.

Index